Prince Consort of England Albert

The principal Speeches and Addresses of His Royal Highness the Prince Consort

With an Introduction giving some Outlines of his Character

Prince Consort of England Albert

The principal Speeches and Addresses of His Royal Highness the Prince Consort
With an Introduction giving some Outlines of his Character

ISBN/EAN: 9783337069421

Printed in Europe, USA, Canada, Australia, Japan

Cover: Foto ©ninafisch / pixelio.de

More available books at **www.hansebooks.com**

THE PRINCIPAL SPEECHES AND ADDRESSES

OF

HIS ROYAL HIGHNESS

THE PRINCE CONSORT.

WITH AN INTRODUCTION, GIVING SOME OUTLINES
OF HIS CHARACTER.

SIXTH THOUSAND.

LONDON:
JOHN MURRAY, ALBEMARLE STREET.
1862.

The right of Translation is reserved.

LONDON: PRINTED BY W. CLOWES AND SONS, STAMFORD STREET,
AND CHARING CROSS.

CONTENTS.

	PAGE
INTRODUCTION	11
THE OFFICE OF COMMANDER-IN-CHIEF	63
SPEECH AT A MEETING FOR THE ABOLITION OF SLAVERY, JUNE 1, 1840	81
SPEECH AT THE LITERARY FUND DINNER, 1842	83
SPEECH AT A MEETING OF THE CORPORATION OF THE TRINITY HOUSE	85
SPEECH AT THE MEETING OF THE SOCIETY FOR IMPROVING THE CONDITION OF THE LABOURING CLASSES, MAY 18, 1848	87
SPEECH AT THE MEETING OF THE ROYAL AGRICULTURAL SOCIETY HELD AT YORK, JULY 13, 1848	91
SPEECH AT THE LAYING OF THE FIRST STONE OF THE GREAT GRIMSBY DOCKS, APRIL 18, 1849	93
SPEECH AT THE PUBLIC MEETING OF THE SERVANTS' PROVIDENT AND BENEVOLENT SOCIETY, MAY 16, 1849	96
SPEECH AT THE ENTERTAINMENT GIVEN BY THE MERCHANT TAILORS' COMPANY, JUNE 11, 1849	103
SPEECH ON PRESENTING COLOURS TO THE 23RD REGIMENT, ROYAL WELSH FUSILIERS, JULY 12, 1849	106
SPEECH AT THE BANQUET GIVEN AT THE MANSION HOUSE TO THE MINISTERS, FOREIGN AMBASSADORS, COMMISSIONERS OF THE EXHIBITION OF 1851, AND MAYORS OF TOWNS, MARCH 21, 1850	109

CONTENTS.

	PAGE
SPEECH AT THE LAYING OF THE FOUNDATION STONE OF THE NATIONAL GALLERY AT EDINBURGH, AUGUST 30, 1850	115
SPEECH AT THE BANQUET GIVEN BY THE LORD MAYOR OF YORK AND MAYORS OF CHIEF TOWNS TO THE LORD MAYOR OF LONDON, OCTOBER 25, 1850	118
SPEECH AT THE DINNER OF THE ROYAL ACADEMY, MAY 3, 1851	126
SPEECH AT THE THIRD JUBILEE OF THE SOCIETY FOR THE PROPAGATION OF THE GOSPEL IN FOREIGN PARTS, JUNE 16, 1851	131
SPEECH AT THE ROYAL AGRICULTURAL SOCIETY'S SHOW AT WINDSOR, JULY 16, 1851	136
SPEECHES AT THE BANQUET AT THE TRINITY HOUSE, JUNE 4, 1853	139
SPEECH AT THE BICENTENARY FESTIVAL OF THE CORPORATION OF THE SONS OF THE CLERGY, MAY 10, 1854	146
SPEECHES AT THE DINNER AT THE TRINITY HOUSE, JUNE 21, 1854	149
SPEECHES AT THE ANNUAL DINNER AT THE TRINITY HOUSE, JUNE 9, 1855	154
SPEECHES AT THE OPENING OF THE NEW CATTLE MARKET, IN COPENHAGEN FIELDS, ISLINGTON, JUNE 13, 1855	159
SPEECHES AT THE BANQUET AT BIRMINGHAM, ON LAYING THE FIRST STONE OF THE BIRMINGHAM AND MIDLAND INSTITUTE, NOVEMBER 22, 1855	162
ADDRESS TO THE 3RD AND 4TH REGIMENTS OF THE GERMAN LEGION AT SHORNCLIFFE, ON PRESENTING TO THEM THEIR COLOURS, DECEMBER 6, 1855	172
SPEECH AT THE OPENING OF THE GOLDEN LANE SCHOOLS, MARCH 19, 1857	173
SPEECHES AT THE OPENING OF THE EXHIBITION OF ART TREASURES AT MANCHESTER, MAY 5, 1857	177

CONTENTS.

	PAGE
SPEECH AT THE OPENING OF THE CONFERENCE ON NATIONAL EDUCATION, JUNE 22, 1857	183
OPENING ADDRESS AT THE MEETING IN THE COLLEGE OF PHYSICIANS FOR THE INAUGURATION OF JENNER'S STATUE, MAY 17, 1858	193
SPEECHES AT THE TRINITY HOUSE, JULY 3, 1858	195
SPEECH AT CHERBOURG, AFTER THE BANQUET ON BOARD 'LA BRETAGNE,' AUGUST 5, 1858	199
SPEECH ON PRESENTING NEW COLOURS TO THE 2ND BATTALION OF THE 13TH ("PRINCE ALBERT'S OWN") LIGHT INFANTRY, AT HARFORD RIDGE, NEAR ALDERSHOT, FEBRUARY 21, 1859	200
SPEECH AT THE MEETING OF THE BRITISH ASSOCIATION FOR THE ADVANCEMENT OF SCIENCE, AT ABERDEEN, SEPTEMBER 14, 1859	203
SPEECH AT THE DINNER ON THE OPENING OF THE CLOTHWORKERS' HALL, IN THE CITY, MARCH 27, 1860	231
SPEECH AT THE BANQUETING ROOM, ST. JAMES'S PALACE, ON THE TWO HUNDREDTH ANNIVERSARY OF THE FORMATION OF THE GRENADIER GUARDS, JUNE 16, 1860	234
SPEECH AT THE DINNER OF THE TRINITY HOUSE, JUNE 23, 1860	243
SPEECH ON OPENING THE INTERNATIONAL STATISTICAL CONGRESS, JULY 16, 1860	250

Two editions of the Prince Consort's Speeches were published by the Society of Arts in 1857; and cheap editions of the same collection have been published since the Prince's death.

The present volume contains, in addition to the speeches previously printed, a speech made by His Royal Highness at the Meeting of the British Association for the Advancement of Science, held at Aberdeen, September 14, 1859; and his address on opening the International Statistical Congress, held in London, 16th July, 1860; together with several minor speeches made by the Prince since the year 1857.

This volume also contains some extracts from a memorandum written by the Prince in reference to the office of Commander-in-Chief.

INTRODUCTION

TO

THE PRINCE CONSORT'S

SPEECHES AND ADDRESSES.

INTRODUCTION.

THE following work contains, with some few trifling exceptions, the speeches and addresses delivered by His Royal Highness the Prince Consort. It is published at the express desire, and under the sanction, of Her Majesty.

It has been thought that this publication will not only be a worthy tribute to the Prince's memory, but that it will have a deep interest for a large circle of readers. There will be those who were personally attached to the Prince, and who will be glad to have a record of these speeches, upon which he bestowed so much care and thought. To the statesman, to the man of science, and to those who care for the social well-being of the people, these speeches will be interesting, as coming from one who himself was a master in those three great

Those who will be interested by the speeches.

branches of human endeavour. And, lastly, to the general student of literature they will possess a high value from the peculiarity of the position of the man who uttered them. Every free and great nation has had, during its best times, a long line of distinguished orators; and, perhaps, the British nation, from its large enjoyment of freedom, may defy the world to compete with it in masterpieces of oratory. The names of Somers, Bolingbroke, Chatham, Burke, Fox, Pitt, Plunket, Grattan, Canning, Sheil, O'Connell, and Macaulay, fill the mind with pictures of attentive listeners, leaning forward, hushed to catch every accent of a great orator speaking upon some great theme. But in every age there will be such men as long as England is a great and free nation. We have them in our senate now; and we feel that there are men living amongst us who are fully worthy to take high places in the illustrious roll of British orators. But, without claiming for the Prince Consort any peculiar gift of oratory, it may fairly be maintained that the world has far more chance of hearing speeches similar to those of even

Peculiarity of the Prince's position.

Great Britain fertile in orators.

the most renowned among the orators just mentioned, than speeches like his; for they were, in their way, unique. It must be a fortunate country indeed, that, even in an extended course of its history, should have two such men, so placed, as the deeply-lamented Prince Consort.

<small>Rarity of speeches like those of the Prince.</small>

Now, why were these speeches unique? In the first place, the man who spoke them had not only a scientific and an artistic mind (which is a rare combination), but he was full of knowledge and of suggestive views upon almost every subject. But that was not all. The expression of this knowledge and of these views had to be compressed and restrained in every direction. He was a Prince, and so close to the Throne that he could not but feel that every word he uttered might be considered as emanating from the Throne. He was not born in the country, and therefore he had to watch lest any advice he gave might be in the least degree unacceptable, as not coming from a native. He had all the responsibilities of office, without having a distinct office to fill. At all points he had to guard himself from envy, from miscon-

<small>The drawbacks upon the Prince in speaking.</small>

struction, and from the appearance of taking too much upon himself. His was a position of such delicacy and difficulty that not one of his contemporaries would presume to think he could have filled it as well as the Prince did. And all this difficulty, and all this delicacy, must have come out in fullest relief before him when he had to make any public utterance.

Eloquence much furthered by absence from restraint.

It is said, and with some truth, that almost anybody might appear witty who should be inconsiderate and unscrupulous in his talk. The gracious reserve that kind-hearted men indulge in, tends to dim their brilliancy, and to lessen their powers of conversation. What is true of wit is true also of wisdom. In considering the speeches of the best speakers, and comparing them one with another, careful account must be taken of the degrees of freedom of speech which the speakers respectively enjoyed. Often a man gains great credit for eloquence and boldness, when the credit is largely due to his having no responsibility, or to his careless way of ignoring what he has. Such considerations as the above should be continually in the mind of any reader of the

Prince Consort's speeches, who may wish to understand them thoroughly, and justly to appreciate the speaker. It has been said that speech is silver, and silence is golden; and if there be anything more precious than gold, it may well be applied to describe that happy mingling of freedom of thought, with a due reserve in the expression of that thought, which ought to mark the speeches of men in an exalted position. They cannot afford to make a speech, however good it may be in the main, that has one needless witticism in it, or the slightest touch of exaggeration, or the least indication of party prejudice.

Of the Prince's speeches, as of much of his life, it may be said that the movement of them was graceful, noble, and dignified; but yet it was like the movement of a man in chain armour, which, even with the strongest and most agile person, must ever have been a movement somewhat fettered by restraint.

The principal elements that go to compose a great oration had often to be modified largely in these speeches of the Prince. Wit was not to be jubilant,—passion not predominant,—dialectic skill not triumphant. There remained nothing as the secure staple of the speech but supreme common sense. Looked at in this way, it is wonderful that the Prince contrived to introduce into his speeches so much that was new and interesting.

After reading continuously the speeches of any remarkable man, we generally seek to discover what is the leading idea of his mind—what is the string on which his pearls of rhetoric, or of fancy, have been strung. And if we were asked what is this leading idea with the Prince, we might safely reply—the beauty of usefulness.

<small>The leading idea of the speaker.</small>

Not that there are not many minor characteristics of an admirable kind which it may be well to point out, and to illustrate by examples. His speeches, though short, are singularly exhaustive of the subject. As an instance, take his speech at the Servants' Provident Benevolent Society. "I "conceive," he said, "that this Society is "founded upon a right principle, as it fol- "lows out the dictates of a correct appre- "ciation of human nature, which requires "every man, by personal exertion and ac-

<small>His speeches exhaustive.</small>

<small>Speech at the Servants' Provident Benevolent Society.</small>

"cording to his own choice, to work out
"his own happiness, which prevents his
"valuing, nay, even feeling satisfaction at,
"the prosperity which others have made
"for him. It is founded on a right prin-
"ciple, because it endeavours to trace out a
"plan, according to which, by providence,
"by self-denial and perseverance, not only
"will the servant be raised in his physical
"and moral condition, but the master also
"will be taught how to direct his efforts in
"aiding the servant in his labour to secure
"to himself resources in case of sickness,
"old age, and want of employment. It is
"founded on a right principle, because in
"its financial scheme there is no temptation
"held out to the servant by the prospect of
"probable extravagant advantages, which
"tend to transform his providence into a
"species of gambling; by convivial meet-
"ings, which lead him to ulterior expense;
"or by the privilege of balloting for the
"few prizes, which draws him into all the
"waste of time and excitement of an
"electioneering contest."

Another striking instance of this exhaustiveness, and also of his generosity of feeling, is to be seen in those passages of his speech at the dinner of the Royal Academy in 1851 where he speaks of criticism. "Gentle-" men," he said, " the production of all works " in art or poetry requires in their concep-" tion and execution not only an exercise " of the intellect, skill, and patience, but " particularly a concurrent warmth of feel-" ing and a free flow of imagination. This " renders them most tender plants, which " will thrive only in an atmosphere calcu-" lated to maintain that warmth, and that " atmosphere is one of kindness towards the " artist personally as well as towards his " productions. An unkind word of criticism " passes like a cold blast over their tender " shoots, and shrivels them up, checking the " flow of the sap which was rising to pro-" duce perhaps multitudes of flowers and " fruit. But still criticism is absolutely " necessary to the development of art, and " the injudicious praise of an inferior work " becomes an insult to superior genius.

"In this respect our times are peculiarly " unfavourable when compared with those " when Madonnas were painted in the se-" clusion of convents; for we have now on

[margin: Speech at the dinner of the Royal Academy, 1851.]

"the one hand the eager competition of a "vast array of artists of every degree of "talent and skill, and on the other, as "judge, a great public, for the greater part "wholly uneducated in art, and thus led by "professional writers who often strive to "impress the public with a great idea of "their own artistic knowledge, by the mer- "ciless manner in which they treat works "which cost those who produced them the "highest efforts of mind or feeling.

"The works of art, by being publicly ex- "hibited and offered for sale, are becoming "articles of trade, following as such the "unreasoning laws of markets and fashion; "and public and even private patronage is "swayed by their tyrannical influence."

How thoroughly the Prince here feels with the artist! At the same time, how he demands the highest order of criticism! What discernment is shown in the comparison between our own time and other times as regards the peculiar circumstances of criticism! And, in the last paragraph, how justly he points out what are the dangers to High Art in the present period! Indeed, this speech, taken as a whole, may claim to be one of the best that have been delivered in our time.

The Prince's desire to get at principles of action.

Again, another characteristic in the Prince's speeches is the evident desire in them to get at the law, or the principle, upon which the matter in question should be settled. As an instance of this I would adduce the following extract from his speech when laying the first stone of the Birmingham and Midland Institute: "Without

Speech on laying the first stone of the Birmingham and Midland Institute.

" such knowledge we are condemned to one
" of three states: either we merely go on to
" do things just as our fathers did, and for
" no better reason than because they did so;
" or, trusting to some personal authority,
" we adopt at random the recommendation
" of some specific in a speculative hope that
" it may answer; or, lastly, and this is the
" most favourable case, we ourselves im-
" prove upon certain processes; but this
" can only be the result of an experience
" hardly earned and dearly bought, and
" which, after all, can only embrace a com-
" paratively short space of time and a small
" number of experiments.

"From none of these courses can we

"hope for much progress; for the mind,
"however ingenious, has no materials to
"work with, and remains in presence of
"phenomena, the causes of which are hidden
"from it.

"But these laws of nature, these divine
"laws, are capable of being discovered and
"understood, and of being taught and made
"our own. This is the task of science:
"and whilst science discovers and teaches
"these laws, art teaches their application.
"No pursuit is therefore too insignificant
"not to be capable of becoming the sub-
"ject both of science and art."

Contrary to our feeling in reading most speeches, we are always sorry when the Prince has ended, and we want more to have been said by him; and yet, if we look attentively at any of the speeches, we cannot but see that so much has been said that we must acknowledge ourselves somewhat unreasonable in wishing to have had any more. His speech on laying the foundation-stone of the National Gallery at Edinburgh affords a notable instance of this. It is so short that you feel inclined to clamour for more; and

Condenseness of the Prince's speeches.

yet, when you read it attentively, you find that enough has been said to make up what would have been a long and telling speech in Parliament. Happily the Prince's absence from the parliamentary arena freed him from that tendency to needless amplification which is the besetting sin even of the best speakers in the present day.

The sympathetic nature of the Prince, which enabled him to feel so largely and deeply for all classes of men, visible throughout his speeches, is nowhere better seen than in his speech at the Bicentenary Festival of the Sons of the Clergy. How rarely, by any one, has a just tenderness for the Clergy been shown in ampler and in nobler terms than in the following extract :—

<small>Speech at the Bicentenary Festival of the Sons of the Clergy.</small>

" Gentlemen, the appellation of a 'money-
" making parson' is not only a reproach
" but a condemnation for a clergyman, de-
" priving him at once of all influence over
" his congregation; yet this man, who has
" to shun opportunities for acquiring wealth
" open to most of us, and who has himself
" only an often scanty life income allotted
" to him for his services, has a wife and

" children like ourselves; and we wish him
" to have the same solicitude for their
" welfare which we feel for our own."

In estimating the Prince Consort's speeches, it is to be recollected that for the most part they treat of topics of an abstract character, and seldom take up what is merely personal as their subject, which, however, is always the most interesting to mankind.

This could not be avoided from the position of the Prince; but it is much to be regretted, for whenever he did speak of something personal, he was particularly successful.

For instance, if we were called upon to furnish for history the main characteristics of Sir Robert Peel's mind, we could not refer to any description of that eminent statesman which would at all compete with that given by the Prince Consort in the speech that he made at the dinner to which he was invited by the Lord Mayor of York.

" There is but one alloy," the Prince said,
" to my feelings of satisfaction and pleasure
" in seeing you here assembled again, and

" that is, the painful remembrance that one
" is missing from amongst us who felt so
" warm an interest in our scheme and took
" so active a part in promoting its success,
" the last act of whose public life was attend-
" ing at the Royal Commission: my admi-
" ration for whose talents and character,
" and gratitude for whose devotion to the
" Queen and private friendship towards
" myself, I feel a consolation in having this
" public opportunity to express.

" Only at our last meeting we were still
" admiring his eloquence and the earnest-
" ness with which he appealed to you to
" uphold, by your exertions and personal
" sacrifices, what was to him the highest
" object, the honour of his country; he
" met you the following day together with
" other commissioners, to confer with you
" upon the details of our undertaking; and
" you must have been struck, as everybody
" has been who has had the benefit of his
" advice upon practical points, with the
" attention, care, and sagacity with which
" he treated the minutest details, proving
" that to a great mind nothing is little,
" from the knowledge that in the moral

" and intellectual as in the physical world
" the smallest point is only a link in that
" great chain, and holds its appointed place
" in that great whole which is governed by
" the Divine Wisdom.

" The constitution of Sir Robert Peel's
" mind was peculiarly that of a statesman,
" and of an English statesman: he was
" liberal from feeling, but conservative
" upon principle; whilst his impulse drove
" him to foster progress, his sagacious mind
" and great experience showed him how
" easily the whole machinery of a state and
" of society is deranged, and how important,
" but how difficult also, it is to direct its
" further development in accordance with
" its fundamental principles, like organic
" growth in nature. It was peculiar to
" him, that, in great things as in small, all
" the difficulties and objections occurred to
" him first; he would anxiously consider
" them, pause, and warn against rash re-
" solutions; but, having convinced himself,
" after a long and careful investigation,
" that a step was not only right to be
" taken, but of the practical mode also of
" safely taking it, it became to him a

" necessity and a duty to take it: all his
" caution and apparent timidity changed
" into courage and power of action, and
" at the same time readiness cheerfully to
" make any personal sacrifice which its
" execution might demand."

The Prince's careful preparation of his speeches.

The foregoing are some of the principal characteristics of the Prince's speeches. It remains only to be said that he thought over them with the greatest care and anxiety. His respect for his audience, and also for his own position, made him always endeavour to give the best thought he could to whatever subject he was treating. He looked upon every occasion he had for speaking as affording him an opportunity of saying something that might be useful for his fellow-countrymen; and he toiled to make that something worthy of him, and worthy of them.

The Prince's speech at the TrinityHouse, June 9, 1855.

The Editor of these Speeches has thought it best to give them without any introductory comments or explanations. One speech, however, brought forth so much misrepresentation, that, in reference to that circumstance, some comment may fitly be made upon it. I allude to the speech which the Prince delivered at a dinner at the Trinity House on the 9th of June, 1855. It is an admirable speech, and in it the Prince spoke out more of his whole mind than perhaps in any other. Let us recall the circumstances. We had met with much disaster in the Crimea. The sickness and death of her soldiers had touched most deeply the heart of the Queen; and the Prince, who was a patriot if ever man was, felt for his country the tenderest anxiety. Now, let us look at the speech. In every line of it may be seen the Prince's intense anxiety to gain support for the Government, and unity of resolve amongst the people.

Why does he dwell upon the power of despotism? Not that he delights to praise despotism, but that he wishes us to see that we have an antagonist whose power we must not venture to underrate. Why does he speak of " constitutional government " being under a heavy trial"? Not that, for a moment, he seeks to decry constitutional government; but because he loves it, is devoted to it, partakes that trial which he points out, and seeks only so to consolidate free government that it may maintain its pre-eminence. How well-chosen are the words he used on the occasion referred to, when he says, "We are engaged with a "mighty adversary, who uses against us "all those wonderful powers which have "sprung up under the generating influence "of our liberty and our civilization, and em- "ploys them with all the force which unity of "purpose and action, impenetrable secresy, "and uncontrolled despotic power give him."

<small>Despotism strong in war.</small>

Is it any new thing to say that despotism is naturally strong in the field, and in the movements of great armies? From the days of Philip of Macedon, down, through those of Louis the Fourteenth, to the Empire of the First Napoleon, has it not been the object of great men in free countries so to consolidate free governments as to give them that force and unity which should enable them to meet the despot in the field upon something like equal terms—equal terms, not as regards men (for freemen always fight well), but as regards organization, which has so much to do with superiority in military affairs?

It seems a needless labour to make any defence of this speech, and a labour somewhat open to the censure conveyed in the proverb that excuse is but a form of accusation; but really the justification in this case is so complete, that it does not come within the meaning of the word "excuse." Every lover of this free country must perceive that its only danger of being worsted in some great contest is a momentary inferiority as regards organization; and we should feel much gratitude to any one who, in an exalted position, has the loving boldness to point out what are our dangers. The Prince asked for confidence in the Government. England gave that confidence, and the cause was won.

<small>Danger from want of organization.</small>

Perhaps the greatest injury that men highly-placed can do their countrymen is to flatter them, and to hide from them any point of weakness that there may be in the nation. We smile at flattery when addressed to private persons, and think it no great harm; but it swells into a mischief of gigantic magnitude when addressed to a nation by those who enjoy its confidence.

<small>The fearful mischief of flattering a nation.</small>

We have not far to look for instances

of nations being brought to the brink of ruin because they have not had public men to tell them stern truths as to the inefficiency of their means, and the unwisdom of their ends. All honour, then, to the man who has the courage, at a critical moment, to tell his countrymen where their peril really lies, and what difficulties they must be prepared to overcome.

A view of the Prince's character.

It may, perhaps, be not unwelcome to the reader, and not inappropriate to the subject, that, as an addition to this Introduction, I should attempt to give some view of the character of the Prince, having had some opportunities of observing him closely during the last year or two of his life, and having since heard and carefully compared what those who knew him best could tell of him. Such an attempt to depict the Prince's character may be useful to the future historian, who has to bring before himself some distinct image of each remarkable man he writes about, and who, for the most part, is furnished with only a superficial description, made up of the ordinary epithets which are attached, in a very haphazard way, to the various qualities of eminent persons by their contemporaries. We really obtain very little notion of a creature so strangely-complex as a man, when we are told of him that he was virtuous, that he was just, that he loved the Arts, and that he was good in all the important relations of life. We still hunger to know what were his peculiarities, and what made him differ from other men; for each man, after all, is a sort of new and distinct creation.

It is a great advantage, in estimating any character, to have a clear idea of the aspect of the person whose character is drawn. There are, fortunately, many portraits of the Prince Consort which possess considerable merit; still there is something about almost every countenance which no portrait can adequately convey, and which must be left to description.

The Prince had a noble presence. His carriage was erect: his figure betokened strength and activity; and his demeanour was dignified. He had a staid, earnest, thoughtful look when he was in a grave

A description of the Prince's personal appearance.

mood; but when he smiled (and this is what no portrait can tell of a man) his whole countenance was irradiated with pleasure; and there was a pleasant sound and a heartiness about his laugh which will not soon be forgotten by those who were wont to hear it.

He was very handsome as a young man; but, as often happens with thoughtful men who go through a good deal, his face grew to be a finer face than the early portraits of him promised; and his countenance never assumed a nobler aspect, nor had more real beauty in it, than in the last year or two of his life.

The character is written in the countenance, however difficult it may be to decipher; and in the Prince's face there were none of those fatal lines which indicate craft or insincerity, greed or sensuality; but all was clear, open, pure-minded, and honest. Marks of thought, of care, of studiousness, were there; but they were accompanied by signs of a soul at peace with itself, and which was troubled chiefly by its love for others, and its solicitude for their welfare.

Perhaps the thing of all others that struck an observer most when he came to see the Prince nearly, was the originality of his mind; and it was an originality divested from all eccentricity. He would insist on thinking his own thoughts upon every subject that came before him; and, whether he arrived at the same results as other men, or gainsaid them, his conclusions were always adopted upon laborious reasonings of his own.

The originality of the Prince.

The next striking peculiarity about the Prince was his extreme quickness—intellectually speaking. He was one of those men who seem always to have all their powers of thought at hand, and all their knowledge readily producible.

The quickness of his intellect.

In serious conversation he was perhaps the first man of his day. He was a very sincere person in his way of talking; so that, when he spoke at all upon any subject, he never played with it: he never took one side of a question because the person he was conversing with had taken the other: and, in fact, earnest discussion was one of his greatest enjoyments. He was very patient

His merits in conversation.

His tolerance of contradiction.

in bearing criticism and contradiction; and, indeed, rather liked to be opposed, so that from opposition he might elicit truth, which was always his first object.

Fond of wit and humour.

He delighted in wit and humour; and, in his narration of what was ludicrous, threw just so much of imitation into it as would enable you to bring the scene vividly before you, without at the same time making his imitation in the least degree ungraceful.

His love of freedom.

There have been few men who have had a greater love of freedom, in its deepest and in its widest sense, than the Prince Consort. Indeed, in this respect he was even more English than the English themselves.

His sense of duty.

A strong characteristic of the Prince's mind was its sense of duty. He was sure to go rigidly through anything he had undertaken to do; and he was one of those few men into whose minds questions of self-interest never enter, or are absolutely ignored, when the paramount obligation of duty is presented to them. If he had been a sovereign prince, and, in a moment of peril, had adopted a form of constitution which was opposed to his inclination or his judgment, he would still have abided by it strictly when quiet times came; and the change, if change there was to be, must have come from the other parties to the contract, and not from him. He was too great a man to wish to rule, if the power was to be purchased by anything having the reality, or even the semblance, of dishonour. It is not too much to say, that, if he had been placed in the position of Washington, he could have played the part of Washington, taking what honour and power his fellow-citizens were pleased to give him, and not asking, or scheming, for any more. He must have sympathized much with the late Duke of Wellington, whose main idea seemed to be to get through life justly and creditably, taking the full measure of responsibility put upon him, and not seeking to have his soul burdened with any more. Such men are absolutely of a different order of mind from the commonplace seekers after power and self-glorification.

The Prince, as all know, was a man of many pursuits and of various accomplishments, with an ardent admiration for the beautiful both in Nature and in Art. Gradually, however, he gave up pursuits that he was fond of, such as the cultivation of music and drawing; not that he relished these pursuits less than heretofore, but that he felt it was incumbent upon him to attend more and more to business. He was not to employ himself upon what specially delighted him, but to attend to what it was his duty to attend to. And there was not time for both.

The Prince gradually gave up some of his favourite pursuits.

Another characteristic of the Prince (which is not always found in those who take a strict view of duty) was his strong aversion to anything like prejudice or intolerance. He loved to keep his own mind clear for the reception of new facts and arguments; and he rather expected that everybody else should do the same. His mind was eminently judicial; and it was never too late to bring him any new view, or fresh fact, which might be made to bear upon the ultimate decision which he would have to give upon the matter. To investigate carefully, weigh patiently, discuss dispassionately, and then, not swiftly, but after much turning over the question in his mind,

The Prince's aversion to prejudice and intolerance.

to come to a decision—was his usual mode of procedure in all matters of much moment.

There was one very rare quality to be noticed in the Prince,—that he had the greatest delight in anybody else saying a fine saying, or doing a great deed. He would rejoice over it, and talk about it, for days; and whether it was a thing nobly said or done by a little child, or by a veteran statesman, it gave him equal pleasure. He delighted in humanity doing well on any occasion and in any manner.

The Prince's delight in the good deeds of other persons.

This is surely very uncommon. We meet with people who can say fine sayings, and even do noble actions, but who are not very fond of dwelling upon the great sayings or noble deeds of other persons. But, indeed, throughout his career, the Prince was one of those who threw his life into other people's lives, and lived in them. And never was there an instance of more unselfish and chivalrous devotion than that of his to his Consort-Sovereign and to his adopted country. That Her reign might be great and glorious; that his adopted country might excel in art, in science, in literature, and, what was dearer still to him, in social well-being, formed ever his chief hope and aim. And he would have been contented to have been very obscure, if these high aims and objects could in the least degree have thereby been furthered and secured.

<small>The Prince's love of his birthplace.</small>

This love of his adopted country did not prevent his being exceedingly attached to his birthplace and his native country. He would recur in the most touching manner, and with childlike joy, to all the reminiscences of his happy childhood. But, indeed, it is clear that, throughout his life, he became in a certain measure attached to every place where he dwelt. This is natural, as he always sought to improve the people and the place where he lived; and so, inevitably, he became attached to it and to them.

A biographer who has some very beautiful character to describe, and who knows the unwillingness that there is in the world to accept, without much qualification, great praise of any human being, will almost be glad to have any small defect to note in his hero. It gives some relief to the picture, and it adds verisimilitude. This defect (if so it can be called) in the Prince consisted in a certain appearance of shyness which he never conquered. And, in truth, it may be questioned whether it is a thing that can be conquered, though large converse with the world may enable a man to conceal it. Much might be said to explain and justify this shyness in the Prince; but there it was, and no doubt it sometimes prevented his high qualities from being at once observed and fully estimated. It was the shyness of a very delicate nature, that is not sure it will please, and is without the confidence and the vanity which often go to form characters that are outwardly more genial.

<small>The Prince's shyness.</small>

<small>The causes of it.</small>

The effect of this shyness was heightened by the rigid sincerity which marked the Prince's character. There are some men who gain much popularity by always expressing in a hearty manner much more than they feel. They are "*delighted*" to see you; they "*rejoice*" to hear that your health is improving; and you, not caring to inquire how much substance there is behind these phrases, and not disinclined to imagine that your health is a matter of importance which people might naturally take interest in, enjoy this hearty but somewhat inflated welcome. But from the Prince there were no phrases of this kind to be had: nothing that was not based upon clear and complete sincerity. Indeed, his refined nature shrank from expressing all it felt, and still less would it condescend to put on any semblance of feeling which was not backed up by complete reality.

<small>The Prince's temperament.</small>

It is very difficult to describe a man's temperament, especially when it is of a somewhat complex nature, as was that of the Prince. It was a buoyant, joyous, happy temperament. It made his home and his household glad. To use a common expression, but a forcible one, he was "the life " and soul of the house." Moreover, the Prince's temperament was very equable, not subject to sudden elations or depressions. To illustrate, however, the complexity, before alluded to, of men's temperaments—beneath this joyousness of the Prince, deep down in the character, there was a vein, not exactly of melancholy, but certainly of pensiveness, which grew a little more sombre as the years went on. It was a pensiveness bred from much pondering upon the difficulty of human affairs, and upon the serious thing that life is.

The writer of this Introduction has often, in his imagination, divided men into two great classes, which seem to him separated by a wide gulf of thought and feeling. The one class is, if it may be so expressed, on the side of humanity: the other is opposed or indifferent to it. This essential difference of character is not necessarily the effect or the concomitant of virtue or of vice, of hopefulness or despondency, of a love of justice or a proneness to injustice; and it has still less to do with any of the intellectual qualities. But it depends upon the presence or the absence of a large and loving nature, where the lovingness takes heed of all humanity. The Prince was pre-eminently one of the first class. He wished for success to all honest human endeavour. No love of criticism, no fondness for paradox, no desire to exalt his own opinion, made him waver in his yearning for the

A division of mankind into two classes.

good of humanity. This caused his intense sympathy with all human work, from that of the artisan to that of the statesman. We have in this age used the word "philan-"thropy" till we are tired of it, till it has become a mawkish word with us; but still there is something very beautiful corresponding to that word, and that was what the Prince possessed. We all recognize in our respective spheres the distinction I have drawn above between these two classes. We all know, for instance, when any public or private disaster happens, who will really grieve over it and endeavour to retrieve it; and who will make it a subject for vain comment, pretended lamentation, or boasting censure. And a nation, like a man, would have come to the Prince when in real trouble, and have found in him one whose sole thought would have been, "what can "now be done for the best?" For he was, as I said before, pre-eminently on the side of humanity, and all that touched other men, touched him, too, very nearly.

The Prince had a horror of flattery. I use the word "horror" advisedly. Dr. Johnson

[Marginalia: The Prince's sympathy for work. The Prince a philanthropist. The Prince helpful in times of trouble. His aversion to flattery.]

somewhere says that flattery shows, at any rate, a desire to please, and may, therefore, be estimated as worth something on that account. But the Prince could not view it in that light. He shuddered at it: he tried to get away from it as soon as he could. It was simply nauseous to him.

He had the same feeling with regard to vice generally. Its presence depressed him, grieved him, horrified him. His tolerance allowed him to make excuses for the vices of individual men; but the evil itself he hated.

His aversion to vice.

What, however, was especially repugnant to the Prince was lowness. He could not bear men to be actuated by low motives. A remarkably unselfish man himself, he scarcely understood selfishness in others; and, when he recognized it, he felt an abhorrence for it. The conditions that the Prince drew up for the prize that is given by Her Majesty at Wellington College are very characteristic of him. This prize is not to be awarded to the most bookish boy, to the least faulty boy, to the boy who should be most precise, diligent, and prudent; but to the noblest boy, to the boy

Low motives odious to him.

who should afford most promise of becoming a large-hearted, high-motived man.

The Prince's religious feelings.

The Prince was a deeply religious man, yet was entirely free from the faintest tinge of bigotry or sectarianism. His strong faith in the great truths of religion coexisted with a breadth of tolerance for other men struggling in their various ways to attain those truths. His views of Religion did not lead him to separate himself from other men; and in these high matters he rather sought to find unity in diversity, than to magnify small differences. Thus he endeavoured to associate himself with all earnest seekers after religious truth.

Some men acquire knowledge without loving it.

It must have occurred to every observer of mankind to notice that there are persons who acquire knowledge without loving it. They have read all the noblest works in literature without being profoundly touched by any of them. They may be excellent classical scholars, and yet they do not seem to love their Horace or their Virgil. Their minds are not penetrated with a sense of the beauty of these authors. They do not see that an idea has been expressed once and for ever, in the choicest language, by these masters of expression: whereas, some humble student perceives all this; and Virgil, Horace, and Ovid belong to him. The same thing occurs in science; the same in law; the same in medicine. You see men who know all about their art, or their science, but who do not seem to love it. They are not led up to all nature by it. It is with them a business, rather than a science or an art. Such was not the case with the Prince. He was singularly impressed with the intellectual beauty of knowledge; for, as he once remarked to Her who most sympathised with him, " To me, a long, closely-connected train " of reasoning is like a beautiful strain " of music. You can hardly imagine my " delight in it." But this was not all with him. He was one of those rare seekers after truth who carry their affections into their acquisitions of knowledge. He loved knowledge on account of what it could do for mankind; and no man of our time sympathized more intimately with that splendid outburst of Bacon, where the great Chancellor exclaims,—

Bacon on knowledge.

"Knowledge is not a couch, whereupon to rest a searching and restless spirit; or a terrace for a wandering and variable mind to walk up and down with a fair prospect; or a tower of state for a proud mind to raise itself upon; or a fort or commanding ground for strife and contention; or a shop for profit or sale; but a rich storehouse for the glory of the Creator, and the relief of man's estate. But this is that which will indeed dignify and exalt knowledge, if contemplation and action may be more nearly and straitly conjoined and united together than they have been; a conjunction like unto that of the two highest planets— Saturn, the planet of rest and contemplation, and Jupiter, the planet of civil society and action."

The Prince's care for the poorer classes.

It was with a feeling similar to that expressed in the foregoing passage that the Prince would comment, for instance, upon an improvement in manufacture, as bearing, especially, upon the health and strength of the poorest classes. It was for "the relief of Man's estate" that this amiable

Prince delighted most in the extension of the bounds of knowledge.

It is always a subject of interest to endeavour to find out how men who have been remarkable for knowledge have found time and opportunity, in this busy, anxious, hurried world, to acquire that knowledge. And in the case of the Prince it is especially difficult to answer the question. But the truth is, that, much as the Prince read books (and in early life he had been very studious), he read men and Nature more. He never gave a listless or half-awake attention to anything that he thought worth looking at, or to any person to whom he thought it worth while to listen. And to the observant man, who is always on the watch for general laws, the minutest objects contemplated by him are full of insight and instruction. In the Prince's converse with men, he delighted at getting at what they knew best, and what they could do. He would always try to get from them the mystery of their craft; and, probably, after the Prince had had an interview with any person of intelligence, that

How the Prince acquired knowledge.

person went away having learnt something from the Prince, and the Prince having learnt something from him. Such men, who are always on the alert to gain and to impart knowledge, deserve to know; and their knowledge soon grows to be beyond book-knowledge, and enters into a higher sphere, as being the result of delicate and attentive observation made by themselves, and for themselves. This is how I account for the Prince's remarkable acquisition of much and various knowledge.

If any man in England cared for the working classes, it was the Prince. He understood the great difficulty of the time as regards these classes; namely, the providing for them fitting habitations. He was a beneficent landlord; and his first care was to build good cottages for all the labouring men on his estates. He had entered into minute calculations as to the amount of illness which might be prevented amongst the poorer classes by a careful selection of the materials to be used in the building of their dwellings. In a word, he was tender, thoughtful, and anxious in his

The Prince's care for the labouring classes.

efforts for the welfare of the labouring man. His constancy of purpose in that, as in other things, was worthy of all imitation. He did not become tired of benevolence. It was not the fancy of a day for him. It was the sustained purpose of a life.

The Prince's love of Art must be spoken of separately, for it was something peculiar to himself. He saw through Art into what, in its highest form, it expressed—the beautiful. He cared not so much for a close representation of the things of daily life, as for that ideal world which Art shadows forth, and interprets to mankind. Hence his love for many a picture which might not be a masterpiece of drawing or of colouring, but which had tenderness and reverence in it, and told of something that was remote from common life, and high and holy.

What he sought for in Art.

Joined with this longing for an interpretation of the ideal, there was in the Prince a love of Art for itself—a pleasure in the skilful execution of a design, whether executed by himself or others. He was no mean artist, and his knowledge of Art stretched forth into various directions. But this was not the remarkable point. There have been other Princes who have been artists. It was in his love of Art—in his keen perception of what Art could do, and of what was its highest province—that he excelled many men who were distinguished artists themselves, and had given their lives to the cultivation of Art.

Skill in organization.

Again, there was the Prince's skill in organization, that almost amounted to an art, which he showed in all the work he touched, and in everything he advised upon.

It may, therefore, justly be said that the Prince approached the highest realms of Art in various ways, which are seldom combined in any one person: in his fondness for what is romantic and ideal, in his love of skill and handicraft, and in his uniform desire for masterly organization.

What the Prince did for agriculture.

In distinguishing the various branches of Art which the Prince devoted himself to, and loved to further, Agriculture must be particularly mentioned, not only on account of the great interest he took in it, and of the practical skill he brought to it, but because of the felicitous results which followed upon his enterprises in this department. As regards works of High Art, it is not much that the wisest Prince, or the most judicious patron, can do to further them. They depend upon the existence, at any particular period, of men or women of genius; and the production of such works lies in a region which is beyond and above the patronage even of the most judicious patrons. But it is not so with Agriculture; and the Prince might fairly lay claim to having himself done much towards that improvement in agriculture which, happily for this country, has been so marked and so rapid within the last twenty years. Men are always much influenced by what their superiors in station do. And that the Prince should have been one of the first persons in this country to appreciate the merits of Deep Drainage, to employ Steam Power in cultivation (a power which does not require to be fed when it is put by in its stable after the day's work), and to apply the resources of Chemistry to Practical Agriculture, ensured the welcome consequence that there would be many followers where the foremost man of England was anxious and ready to lead the way. That, with a large breadth of the lands of Great Britain partially tilled, or scarcely cultivated at all, the British Nation should not unfrequently have to expend twenty or thirty millions of money in foreign corn, is a reproach against our practical sagacity, in which the Prince at least can have no share of the blame.

It has been said that, if we knew any man's life intimately, there would be some great and peculiar moral to be derived from it—some tendency to be noted, which other men, observing it in his career, might seek to correct in themselves. I cannot help thinking that I see what may be the moral to be derived from a study of the Prince's life. It is one which applies only to a few amongst the highest natures; and, simply stated, it is this—that he cared too much about too many things.

The Prince too much interested in too many things.

His craving for perfection.

Moreover, everything in which he was concerned must be done supremely well if it was to please and satisfy him. The great German, Goethe, had the same defect, or rather the same superabundance. He would take inordinate pains even in writing a short note, that it should be admirably written. He did not understand the merit of second-best; but everything that was to be done must be done perfectly. It was thus with the Prince. In the choice of a jewel, in the placing of a statue, in the laying out of a walk, in the direction of a party of pleasure, his reasoning mind must be satisfied; and he longed that everything that was to be, should be the best of its kind.

Now men of this nature, with an abiding aspiration towards what is beautiful, and such an inordinate appreciation of what is reasonable, require also to have an extraordinary stock of health,* otherwise they make extravagant demands upon their powers of thought and attention, and thus upon the primary elements of life.

Strain upon the health.

---

* And the Prince had very good health. At any rate he had begun with a fine constitution. Every one of the chief organs of life was well developed in him, with the exception of a heart that was not quite equal to the work put upon it; so that he mostly had but a feeble pulse. It was upon the nervous energy that this constant stress of work, and this striving after excellence in everything, must have told, as such demands do tell upon all men of that high nature.

The man who insists upon having a good reason for everything he thinks and does, has set himself a task which it requires almost superhuman energy to master. With a boundless appetite for knowledge, the Prince declined to be superficial in anything; and whatever question was brought to him, he set to work at it with a resolution to give his best attention to solve it. All men, when they find such a mind to lean upon, delight to bring their difficulties to it; and in the Prince's case his extraordinary good nature and prompt sympathy forbade him to ignore any question which interested his fellow-men. I cannot help thinking that, but for this peculiarity in his nature—a peculiarity which, regret it as we may, we cannot but love and admire—he would have lived for many years longer, to be, as he had always been, the worthiest and ablest supporter of the Throne, and the foremost advocate of all that held out a promise of increasing the welfare of the people.

It may here be well to remind the reader that the Prince was only forty-two years of age when he died; and that the sagacity and prudence for which he gained a just renown, were manifested at an age when many other men, even of the brightest sort, are far from showing maturity of judgment. This early death, too, makes the great amount of knowledge that he had acquired all the more extraordinary. And, altogether, we may say that seldom has there been compressed into a life more of thought, energy, and anxious care, than was crowded into his. His death appears especially premature at a period when we are accustomed to have great soldiers, lawyers, and statesmen distinguishing themselves, and almost showing new faculties, after they have reached the threescore years and ten so pathetically spoken of by the Psalmist. If the Prince had lived to attain what we now think a good old age, he would inevitably have become the most accomplished statesman and the most guiding personage in Europe—a man to whose arbitrement fierce national quarrels might have been submitted, and by whose influence calamitous wars might have been averted.

So subtly are men constituted, and so difficult is it, even from a careful enumeration of their qualities, to get at the result of their nature, and to understand the men themselves, that it would be possible, notwithstanding all that has been justly said in praise of the Prince, that he might still have failed to be a very loveable character. You meet with people against whom nothing in dispraise can well be urged, and for whom high-sounding panegyrics might justly be written, who yet are not pleasant, amiable, or loveable. It was not so, however, with the Prince. The mere enumeration of his high qualities and his good tendencies would fail to give a just representation of his peculiarly gentle, tender, and pathetic cast of mind. Indeed this kind of character is rather German than English, and had always been much noted as a prevailing character in the Prince's family. Though eminently practical, and therefore suited to the people he came to dwell amongst, he had in a high degree that gentleness, that softness, and that romantic nature, which belong to his race and his nation, and which make them very pleasant to live with, and very tender in all their social and family relations.

The gentleness of the Prince.

Finally there was in the Prince a quality which I think may be noticed as belonging to most men of genius and of mark. I mean a certain childlike simplicity. It is noticed of such men that, mentally speaking, they do not grow old like other men. There is always a playfulness about them, a certain innocency of character, and a power of taking interest in what surrounds them, which we naturally associate with the beauty of youthfulness. It is a pity to use a foreign word if one can help it, but it illustrates the character of such men to say that they never can become "*blasés*." Those who had the good fortune to know the Prince, will, I am sure, admit the truth of this remark as applied to him; and will agree in the opinion that neither disaster, sickness, nor any other form of human adversity, would have been able to harden his receptive nature, or deaden his soul to the wide-spread interests of humanity. He would always have been young in heart; and a great proof of this was his singular attractiveness to all those about him who were young.

<small>The abiding youthfulness of men of genius possessed by him.</small>

One gift that the Prince possessed, which

tended to make him a favourite with the young, was his peculiar aptitude for imparting knowledge. Indeed, the skill he showed in explaining anything, whether addressed to the young or the old, ensured the readiest attention; and it would not be easy to find, even among the first Professors and Teachers of this age, any one who could surpass the Prince in giving, in the fewest words, and with the least use of technical terms, a lucid account of some difficult matter in science which he had mastered—mastered not only for himself, but for all others who had the advantage of listening to him.

The one of his children who was most capable of judging of what his conduct had been to all his children as a father and a friend, speaks thus of him:—

" But in no relation of life did the
" goodness and greatness of his character
" appear more than in the management
" of his children. The most judicious,
" impartial, and loving of fathers, he was
" at once the friend and master, ever by
" his example enforcing the precepts he
" sought to instil."

The Prince's marriage was singularly felicitous. The tastes, the aims, the hopes, the aspirations of the Royal Pair were the same. Their mutual respect and confidence went on increasing. Their affection grew, if possible, even warmer and more intense as the years of their married life advanced. Companions in their domestic employments, in their daily labours for the State, and, indeed, in almost every occupation,—the burthens and the difficulties of life were thus lessened more than by half for each one of the persons thus happily united in this true marriage of the soul. When the fatal blow was struck, and the Prince was removed from this world, it is difficult to conceive a position of greater sorrow, and one, indeed, more utterly forlorn, than that which became the lot of the Survivor—deprived of him whom She Herself has described as being the "Life of Her Life."

The Prince's marriage.

To follow out his wishes—to realize his hopes — to conduct his enterprizes to a happy issue—to make his loss as little felt as possible by a sorrowing country and fatherless children :—these are the objects which, since his death, it has been the chief aim and intent of Her Majesty to accomplish. That strength may be given her to fulfil these high purposes, is the constant prayer of her subjects, who have not ceased, from the first moment of her bereavement, to feel the tenderest sympathy for her; and who, giving a reality to that which in the case of most Sovereigns is but a phrase, have thus shown that the Queen is indeed, in their hearts, the Mother of her people.

<small>How the Prince was mourned for.</small> It is a matter of history that, at the untimely end of the Prince, the sorrow of the whole nation went with him to his grave. That was due to his great public qualities: but, within a narrower circle, the endearing qualities of his nature called forth a deeper anguish and a more abiding affliction. Never was there a man more mourned by his family, by his friends, by those of his household, and by all persons who had come into contact or connection with him. This is perhaps the most favourable trait, the most undeniable proof of goodness and of greatness of heart, that can be brought

forward of any man; for though we read upon tombstones of the undying regret of family and friends, it is in reality given to few amongst the sons of men to leave a blank in the lives of many other persons, which refuses to be filled up—a fond and passionate regret which may be soothed, but which, in their devoted hearts, can never be effaced.

NOTE.

It must be obvious to the reader of this Introduction that the writer has received the most valuable and important aid from those who, by their constant intercourse with the Prince Consort, could best appreciate the high qualities which shone forth in his domestic life—from persons in the Royal Household who saw him daily—from Members of the Royal Family—and especially from the Queen Herself. To Her Majesty the writer is indebted for a view of the Prince's character in which a loving and profound appreciation is combined with the most earnest desire for exact truth and faithfulness. There is not any one who could have been cognizant of all the various traits of the Prince enumerated in this Introduction, unless he had been instructed by Her, who alone saw, with the full light of a complete affection, into the whole beauty and merit of the character of this remarkable Man.

LONDON,
October, 1862.

THE OFFICE

OF

COMMANDER-IN-CHIEF.

THE foregoing is simply an Introduction to the Prince Consort's Speeches, with some outlines of the Prince's character. It is in no respect meant to anticipate the publication of his Life; and, consequently, no documents have been inserted, or even alluded to, which would be required for the illustration of that life.

One exception, however, to this rule the Queen has graciously consented to make. Amongst the manuscripts left by the Prince, there is a memorandum in his own handwriting on a subject of great importance in itself. But now, alas! the memorandum is of more importance still, as illustrating, in a remarkable manner, the Prince's character and conduct. In this document he clearly defines his own position, and lays out as it were the main scheme and purpose of his life. His words on this occasion are like a lamp raised up high on a vessel, which casts long lines of light upon the waves before and after, showing the course which has been passed over, and that which will be passed over, as the ship speeds right onwards through the dark waters of the uncertain sea.

In the Introduction a character has been drawn, which might be cavilled at from its having so much that is bright in it, and so little that affords any contrast whatever of darkness. The Prince is there depicted as a most self-denying man. Those who lived with him knew that it was so; they knew that the habit of self-denial pervaded his whole life. But it might be difficult for the rest of the world to be assured of the full extent of this self-denial.

After reading the document in question, there will no longer be any doubt upon this point. It can hardly be imagined that anything could be more tempting to a young man, placed as the Prince was, than to have almost within his grasp such a grand and distinct position as that of the Commander-in-Chief of the British Army. Throughout the memorandum it is evident that the Prince felt the temptation deeply while he abjured it. It was not the cold refusal of a person indifferent to what was offered to him; but it was the stern self-sacrifice of one who, abounding in noble ambition, would dearly like to take the honour and the labour which he feels it his duty to decline.

The circumstances portrayed in the memorandum are very dramatic, and are exceedingly interesting, if only on that account. We cannot but picture to ourselves the tender wife already but too justly anxious for her Consort's health; the aged Duke, with his well-known and long-tried devotion to the Throne, urging, in his decided manner, upon the Prince the acceptance of this much-coveted post; and the Prince modestly and decisively putting it from him as a thing he must not have. There was wisdom in the motives which led the old warrior and statesman to make the proposal. But there was a higher wisdom in those of the young Prince who steadily refused to entertain the offer: a wisdom not proceeding from a nice perception of what was safe for self-interest, or from a skilful balancing of consequences, but from an instinct of goodness cultivated by chivalry into the highest self-devotion.

The resolution which the Prince announces in this memorandum — to sink his own individual existence in that of the Queen—had long been acted upon by him even then, and was never afterwards departed from. It was not repented of: it gave a colour to his whole career: it sustained him in long days of wearisome, commonplace labour: it became a part of his being; and he never surrendered it but with his last breath.

Many a reader of the foregoing Introduction, not having met with anything like the Prince's character in ordinary life, might naturally imagine it to have been drawn by too partial a hand. But this thought will vanish, when he sees the Prince unconsciously depicted by himself, and thus learns, from undoubted authority, what was the object, what the meaning, and what the settled purpose of his well-spent life.

In allowing this Memorandum of the Prince to be published, the Queen is also actuated by another motive in addition to those which have already been mentioned. It affords Her Majesty a fitting opportunity for expressing, in the most clear and ample manner, that which for many years she has desired to express. During the Prince's life, the Queen often longed to make known to the world the ever-present, watchful, faithful, invaluable aid which she received from the Prince Consort in the conduct of the public business. Her Majesty could hardly endure even then to be silent on this subject, and not to declare how much her Reign owed to him. And now the Queen can no longer refrain from uttering what she has so long felt, and from proclaiming the irreparable loss to the public service, as well as to herself and to her family, which the Prince's death has occasioned.

The position of Her Majesty, for many years accustomed to this loving aid, and now suddenly bereft of it, can with difficulty be imagined to the full extent of its heaviness and its sadness. Desolate and sombre, as the Queen most deeply feels, lies the way before her ;—a path, however, of duty and of labour, which, relying on the loyal attachment and sympathy of her people, she will, with God's blessing, strive to pursue; but where she fears her faltering steps will often show they lack the tender and affectionate support which, on all occasions, Her Majesty was wont to receive from her beloved husband, the Prince.

The circumstances which preceded the drawing up of this Memorandum by the Prince, are as follows :—

On the death of Sir J. Macdonald, the Adjutant-General, in March, 1850, a suggestion was made to amalgamate the two offices of Adjutant and Quartermaster-General under a single head, to be called Chief of the Staff. The Duke of Wellington was in consequence summoned to Windsor, and several conversations ensued, in the course of which the Duke proposed that arrangements should be made with a view to the Prince's ultimately succeeding himself as Commander-in-Chief.*

The following are extracts from the minutes made by the Prince of those conversations, as far as they related to that proposal :—

Windsor Castle, April 3, 1850.

I went yesterday to see the Duke of Wellington in his room after his arrival at the Castle,

---

* The circumstances narrated above, and the conduct of the Prince Consort upon them, were related by Earl Russell very succinctly and accurately in his speech in the House of Commons, Jan. 31, 1854.

our conversation soon turning to the question of the vacant Adjutant-Generalship. I asked the Duke what he was prepared to recommend. He said he had had a letter on the subject recommending the union of the two offices of Adjutant-General and Quartermaster-General, and he placed his answer to it in my hands. He then proceeded to say that he thought it necessary that we should cast our eyes a little before us. He was past 80 years, and would next month enter upon his 82nd. He was, thank God! very well and strong, and ready to do anything; but he could not last for ever, and in the natural course of events we must look to a change ere long. As long as he was there, he did the duty of all the offices himself. . . . . To form a new office by uniting the duties of Adjutant-General and Quartermaster-General in the person of a Chief of the Staff, as was the practice in some foreign armies, would be to appoint two different persons to do the same duty, which would never answer. The Chief of the Staff would again have to subdivide his office into an Adjutant-General and Quartermaster-General's Department, and nothing would be gained.

However, the Duke saw the greatest advantage in having a Chief of the Staff, if, after his death, that arrangement should be made which he had always looked to, and which he considered the best, viz. *that I should assume the command of the army.*

He was sure I could not do it without such a Chief of the Staff, who would be responsible before the public, and carry on the official communications with the other Government Departments. For this contingency he was prepared to organize the machinery now, and he would answer for its success. . . . .

I answered to the Duke that I should be very slow to make up my mind to undertake so great a responsibility — that I was not sure of my fitness for it, on account of my want of military experience, &c. (to which the Duke replied, that with good honest intentions one could do a great deal, and that he should not be the least afraid on that score) — whether I could perform the duties consistently with my other avocations, as I should not like to undertake what I could not carry through, not knowing what time or attention they would require.

The Duke answered, that it would certainly require both time and attention, for nothing could be done without my knowledge, or without my order, but that the detail would be worked out by the Chief of the Staff. He had thoroughly considered that, and would make it work. . . . He always stood up for the principle of the army being commanded by the Sovereign; and he endeavoured to make the practice agree with that theory, by scrupulously taking, on every point, the Queen's pleasure before he acted. But, were he gone, he saw no security, unless I undertook the command myself, and thus supplied what was deficient in the constitutional working of the theory, arising from the circumstance of the present Sovereign being a lady. Strictly constitutionally I should certainly be responsible for my acts, but before the world in general the Chief of the Staff would bear the responsibility, and for that office the man of the greatest name and weight in the army ought to be selected. He repeated that he thought this the most desirable arrangement, and would at once work it out to the best of his ability. . . . I begged him to leave me time to consider the proposal.

In the evening the Queen gave the Duke of Wellington an audience, I being present. After having set out by saying he was most anxious to let the Queen know and feel all he knew and felt about it—in fact, to *think aloud*—the Duke repeated what he had said to me in the morning, and we discussed the question further. I said that there were several points which still required to be considered. . . . The offer was so tempting for a young man, that I felt bound to look most closely to all the objections to it, in order to come to a right decision. . . . The Queen, as a lady, was not able at all times to perform the many duties imposed upon her; moreover she had no Private Secretary who worked for her, as former Sovereigns had had. The only person who helped her, and who could assist her, in the multiplicity of work which ought to be done by the Sovereign, was myself. I should be very sorry to undertake any duty which would absorb my time and attention so much for *one* Department, as to interfere with my general usefulness to the Queen. . . . The Queen added, that I already worked harder than she liked to see, and than she thought was good for my health,* which I did not allow—answering, that, on the contrary, business must naturally increase with time, and ought to increase, if the Sovereign's duties to the country were to be thoroughly performed; but that I was anxious no more should fall upon her than could be helped.

The Duke seemed struck with this consideration, and said he had not overlooked it, but might not have given it all the weight it deserved, and that he would reflect further upon it.

We agreed at last that this question could not be satisfactorily solved unless we knew the exact

---

* The anxiety of the Queen lest the Prince should injure his health by his excessive attention to public business, naturally continued to increase.

In 1860, when the Society of Arts renewed the proposal for holding a second International Exhibition, the Queen wrote to Lord Granville, without the knowledge of the Prince, expressing Her earnest hope that he (Lord Granville) would do all that in him lay to prevent the responsibility and labour of conducting the undertaking being thrown in any way on His Royal Highness.

The Queen felt deeply the necessity for averting any addition to the heavy work already entailed on the Prince by the assistance and support (every day more needful to Her) which he gave Her in the transaction of all public business; and Her Majesty was convinced that he could not again undertake the labour he had gone through in conducting the first Exhibition to its successful termination, without injury to that health which was not only most precious to Herself and his family, but to the country, and even to the world.

duties which had to be performed; and the Queen charged the Duke to draw up a memorandum in which these should be detailed, and his general opinion explained, so that we might found a decision on that paper. This the Duke promised to do.

Windsor Castle, April 6, 1850.

After a good deal of reflection on the Duke of Wellington's proposal, I went to pay him a visit yesterday morning in his room, and found him prepared with his memorandum, which he handed to me. After having read it, I said to him that I must consider my position as a whole, which was that of the consort and confidential adviser and assistant of a female sovereign. Her interest and good should stand foremost, and all other considerations must be viewed in reference to this, and in subordination to it. The question then was simply, whether I should not weaken my means of attending to all parts of the constitutional position alike—political, social, and moral—if I devoted myself to a special branch, however important that might be; and that I was afraid this would be the consequence of my becoming Commander-in-Chief. It was quite true that the Sovereign being a lady naturally weakened her relation to the army, and that the duty rested upon me of supplying that deficiency, and would do so still more when the protection which the Duke afforded to the Crown should be unfortunately withdrawn. But I doubted whether this might not be accomplished without my becoming especially responsible for the command of the army. There was no branch of public business in which I was not now supporting the Queen, &c. &c. . . . . The Duke replied he quite saw that my position ought to be looked at as a whole. He felt the extreme difficulty and delicacy of it, and was kind enough to add that he approved of, and the public did full justice to the way in which I had hitherto maintained it. I begged him to leave me a little time for consideration, that I wanted to study his memorandum, and would finally write to him upon the subject.

Two days afterwards the Prince wrote to the Duke a letter, of which the following are extracts :—

My dear Duke,

The Queen and myself have thoroughly considered your proposal to join the offices of Adjutant-General and Quartermaster-General into one of a Chief of the Staff, with a view to facilitate the future assumption of the command of the army by myself. . . . . The question whether it will be advisable that I should take the command of the army or not, has been most anxiously weighed by me, and I have come to the conclusion that my decision ought entirely and solely to be guided by the consideration, whether it would interfere with, or assist, my position of Consort of the Sovereign, and the performance of the duties which this position imposes upon me.

This position is a most peculiar and delicate one. Whilst a female sovereign has a great many disadvantages in comparison with a king, yet, if she is married, and her husband understands and does his duty, her position, on the other hand, has many compensating advantages, and, in the long run, will be found even to be stronger than that of a male sovereign. But this requires that the husband should entirely sink his *own individual* existence in that of his wife —that he should aim at no power by himself or for himself—should shun all ostentation—assume no separate responsibility before the public —but make his position entirely a part of hers— fill up every gap which, as a woman, she would naturally leave in the exercise of her regal functions — continually and anxiously watch every part of the public business, in order to be able to advise and assist her at any moment, in any of the multifarious and difficult questions or duties brought before her, sometimes international, sometimes political, or social, or personal. As the natural head of her family, superintendent of her household, manager of her private affairs, sole *confidential* adviser in politics, and only assistant in her communications with the officers of the government, he is besides the husband of the Queen, the tutor of the Royal children, the private secretary of the Sovereign, and her permanent minister.

How far would it be consistent with this position to undertake the management and administration of a most important branch of the public service, and the individual responsibility attaching to it—becoming an Executive Officer of the Crown, receiving the Queen's commands through her Secretaries of State, &c. &c.? I feel sure that, having undertaken the responsibility, I should not be satisfied to leave the business and real work in the hands of another (the Chief of the Staff), but should feel it my duty to look to them myself. But whilst I should in this manner perform duties which, I am sure, every able General Officer, who has gained experience in the field, would be able to perform better than myself, who have not had the advantage of such experience, most important duties connected with the welfare of the Sovereign would be left unperformed, which nobody *could* perform but myself. I am afraid, therefore, that I must discard the tempting idea of being placed in command of the British Army.

SPEECHES

OF

HIS ROYAL HIGHNESS

THE

PRINCE CONSORT.

SPEECHES.

AT A MEETING FOR THE ABOLITION OF SLAVERY.

[JUNE 1st, 1840.]

I HAVE been induced to preside at the Meeting of this Society, from a conviction of its paramount importance to the great interests of humanity and justice.

I deeply regret that the benevolent and persevering exertions of England to abolish that atrocious traffic in human beings (at once the desolation of Africa and the blackest stain upon civilized Europe) have not as yet led to any satisfactory conclusion. But I sincerely trust that this great country will not relax in its efforts until it has finally, and for ever, put an end to a state of things so repugnant to the spirit of Christianity, and the best feelings of our nature.

Let us therefore trust that Providence will prosper our exertions in so holy a cause, and that (under the auspices of our Queen and Her Government) we may at no distant period be rewarded by the accomplishment of the great and humane object for the promotion of which we have this day met.

LITERARY FUND, 1842.

1.

I PROPOSE the health of the Queen, who highly appreciates the tendency of this Institution, and sincerely interests herself in its welfare.

"THE QUEEN, OUR MUNIFICENT PATRON."

2.

I return you my warmest thanks for the great kindness with which you have received this toast. It will always be most gratifying to my feelings to contribute in the smallest degree towards the welfare of any of the excellent Institutions which so prominently distinguish this country.

3.

The toast which I have now to propose to you is the Prosperity of this Institution.

It stands unrivalled in any country, and ought to command our warmest sympathies, as providing for the exigencies of those who, following the call of Genius, and forgetting every other consideration, pursue merely the cultivation of the human mind and science. What can then be more proper for us than gratefully to remember the benefits derived from their disinterested exertions, and cheerfully to contribute to their wants?

I conclude with the ardent wish that the object for which we have this day met will be answered in the most ample and generous way.

"Prosperity to this Institution."

4.

I am sure you will all gladly join me in drinking the health of our worthy President the Marquis of Lansdowne. He would not wish me to enumerate his merits as a patron of the Arts and Science, so well known to this assembly; but it is a satisfaction to me to have an opportunity of expressing how much I esteem them.

"Our President."

THE CORPORATION OF TRINITY HOUSE.

WITH much sincerity I return you my best thanks for the toast which has just been drunk.

I feel a pride in the cause which makes me a guest this day with the Corporation of the Trinity House, to whose exertions in the discharge of your important duties this great country is so deeply indebted.

That these exertions, upon which not only the good of the Mercantile Marine depends, but which have so essentially contributed to the welfare of the Navy, may in their various and important branches be always crowned with success, I warmly wish; and I cannot refrain from expressing how happy I should feel if by my admission into your Corporation I should ever be afforded the smallest opportunity of forwarding any of your objects.

The distinguished honour conferred upon me this day, an honour aspired to and prized by eminent men of every age, will always be held in my most lively remembrance.

[When the heart flies out before the understanding, it saves the judgment a world of pains.]

AT THE MEETING OF THE

SOCIETY FOR IMPROVING THE CONDITION OF THE LABOURING CLASSES.

[MAY 18TH, 1848.]

LADIES AND GENTLEMEN,—

WHEN four years since this Society for the Improvement of the Condition of the Labouring Classes was first established on its present footing, I accepted with great pleasure the offer of becoming its President.

I saw in this offer a proof of your appreciation of my feelings of sympathy and interest for that class of our community which has most of the toil, and least of the enjoyments, of this world. I conceived that great advantage would accrue from the endeavours of influential persons, who were wholly disinterested, to act the part of a friend to those who required that advice and assistance which none but a friend could tender with advantage.

This Society has always held this object before

its eyes, and has been labouring in that direction. You are all aware that it has established model lodging-houses, loan-funds, and the system of allotments of ground in different parts of the country; but it has been careful only to establish examples and models, mindful that any real improvement which was to take place must be the result of the exertions of the working people themselves.

I have just come from the model lodging-house, the opening of which we celebrate this day; and I feel convinced that its existence will, by degrees, cause a complete change in the domestic comforts of the labouring classes, as it will exhibit to them, that with real economy can be combined advantages with which few of them have hitherto been acquainted; whilst it will show to those who possess capital to invest, that they may do so with great profit and advantage to themselves, at the same time that they are dispensing those comforts to which I have alluded, to their poorer brethren.

Depend upon it, the interests of classes too often contrasted are identical, and it is only ignorance which prevents their uniting for each other's advantage. To dispel that ignorance, to show how man can help man, notwithstanding the complicated state of civilized society, ought to be the aim of every philanthropic person; but it is more peculiarly the duty of those who, under the blessing of Divine Providence, enjoy station, wealth, and education.

Let them be careful, however, to avoid any dictatorial interference with labour and employment, which frightens away capital, destroys that freedom of thought and independence of action which must remain to every one if he is to work out his own happiness, and impairs that confidence under which alone engagements for mutual benefit are possible.

God has created man imperfect, and left him with many wants, as it were to stimulate each to individual exertion, and to make all feel that it is only by united exertions and combined action that these imperfections can be supplied, and these wants satisfied. This presupposes self-reliance and confidence in each other. To show the way how these individual exertions can be directed with the greatest benefit, and to foster that confidence upon which the readiness to assist each other depends, this Society deems its most sacred duty.

There has been no ostentatious display of charity or munificence, nor the pretension of becoming the arbiter of the fate of thousands, but the quiet working out of particular schemes of social improvement; for which, however, as I said before, the Society has only established examples for the community at large to follow.

The report of the proceedings of last year will now be laid before you.

I must say—I hope I may say—that the Society has proceeded satisfactorily towards the accomplishment of its objects; and that is owing particularly to the kind feelings, the great experience, and undoubted zeal of Lord Ashley.

The next step which we contemplate taking is the erection of a model lodging-house for families. I have no doubt that the meeting will enable us to carry out that step, and that the attention of the public will be more generally directed to the objects which we have in view.

AT THE MEETING OF

THE ROYAL AGRICULTURAL SOCIETY.

[HELD AT YORK, JULY 13th, 1848.]

Gentlemen,—

I HAVE to thank you most sincerely for your having drunk my health with so much cordiality. It has been a great satisfaction to me to have been able this year to pay an old debt in appearing at this interesting and useful meeting.

All I have seen to-day exhibits a bright picture of the progress of British agriculture, and for much of this progress the country is indebted to this Society.

Agriculture, which was once the main pursuit of this as of every other nation, holds even now, notwithstanding the development of commerce and manufactures, a fundamental position in the realm; and although time has changed the position which the owner of the land, with his feudal dependants, held in the empire, the country gentleman with his wife and children, the country clergyman, the tenant, and the labourer, still form a great, and I hope united, family, in which we gladly recognize the foundation of our social state.

Science and mechanical improvement have in these days changed the mere practice of cultivating the soil into an industrial pursuit, requiring capital, machinery, industry, and skill, and perseverance in the struggle of competition. This is another great change, but we must consider it a great *progress*, as it demands higher efforts and a higher intelligence.

Conscious of these changes, we Agriculturists of England assemble together in this annual meeting of the Royal Agricultural Society, in order to communicate to each other our various experiences, to exhibit the progress that some may have made in the applications of science, and others in the adaptation of machinery, or in the successful rearing of animals.

Feeling, as I do, a great interest in these noble pursuits and their paramount importance, and having myself experienced the pleasures and the little pangs attending them, I feel highly gratified that it should have been confided to me to propose to you the toast of the day, " Success to " the Royal Agricultural Society of England;" and I trust that you will heartily respond to it.

AT THE LAYING THE FIRST STONE
OF THE
GREAT GRIMSBY DOCKS.

[APRIL 18TH, 1849.]

My Lord,*—

I THANK you most sincerely for the kind terms in which you have proposed my health, and you, gentlemen, for the cordial manner in which you have received it.

The act which has this day been performed, and in which you were kind enough to desire that I should take the chief part, could not but make a deep impression upon me.

We have been laying the foundation not only of a Dock, as a place of refuge, safety, and refitment for mercantile shipping, and calculated even to receive the largest steamers in Her Majesty's Navy, but it may be, and I hope it will be, the foundation of a great commercial port, destined in after times, when we shall long have quitted this scene, and when our names even may be forgotten, to form another centre of life to the

* The late Earl of Yarborough, Lord Lieutenant of the county of Lincoln.

vast and ever-increasing commerce of the world, and an important link in the connection of the East and the West. Nay, if I contemplate the extraordinary rapidity of development which characterizes the undertakings of this age, it may not even be too much to expect that some of us may live yet to see this prospect in part realized.

This work has been undertaken, like almost all the national enterprises of this great country, by *private* exertion, with *private* capital, and at *private* risk; and it shares with them likewise that other feature so peculiar to the enterprises of Englishmen, that, strongly attached as they are to the institutions of their country, and gratefully acknowledging the protection of those laws under which their enterprises are undertaken and flourish, they love to connect them, in some manner, directly with the authority of the Crown and the person of their Sovereign; and it is the appreciation of this circumstance which has impelled me at once to respond to your call, as the readiest mode of testifying to you how strongly Her Majesty the Queen values and reciprocates this feeling.

I have derived an additional gratification from this visit, as it has brought me for the first time to the county of Lincoln, so celebrated for its agricultural pursuits, and showing a fine example of the energy of the national character, which has, by dint of perseverance, succeeded in transforming unhealthy swamps into the richest and most fertile soil in the kingdom. I could not have witnessed finer specimens of Lincolnshire farming than have been shown to me on his estates by your Chairman, my noble host, who has made me acquainted, not only with the agricultural improvements which are going on amongst you, but with that most gratifying state of the relation between Landlord and Tenant which exists here, and which I hope may become an example, in time to be followed throughout the country. Here it is that the real advantage and the prosperity of both do not depend upon the written letter of agreements, but on that mutual trust and confidence which has in this country for a long time been held a sufficient security to both, to warrant the extensive outlay of capital, and the engagement in farming operations on the largest scale.

Let me, in conclusion, propose to you as a toast, " Prosperity to the Great Grimsby Docks;" and let us invoke the Almighty to bestow His blessing on this work, under which alone it can prosper.

AT THE PUBLIC MEETING OF THE

SERVANTS' PROVIDENT AND BENEVOLENT SOCIETY.

[MAY 16TH, 1849.]

GENTLEMEN,—

THE object for which we have assembled here to-day is not one of charity, but of friendly advice and assistance to be tendered to a large and important class of our fellow-countrymen.

Who would not feel the deepest interest in the welfare of their Domestic Servants? Whose heart would fail to sympathize with those who minister to us in all the wants of daily life, attend us in sickness, receive us upon our first appearance in this world, and even extend their cares to our mortal remains, who live under our roof, form our household, and are a part of our family?

And yet upon inquiry we find that in this metropolis the greater part of the inmates of the workhouse are domestic servants.

I am sure that this startling fact is no proof

either of a want of kindness and liberality in masters towards their servants, or of vice in the latter, but is the natural consequence of that peculiar position in which the domestic servant is placed, passing periods during his life in which he shares in the luxuries of an opulent master, and others in which he has not even the means of earning sufficient to sustain him through the day.

It is the consideration of these peculiar vicissitudes which makes it the duty of both masters and servants to endeavour to discover and to agree upon some means for carrying the servant through life, safe from the temptations of the prosperous, and from the sufferings of the evil day. It is on that account that I rejoice at this meeting, and have gladly consented to take the chair at it, to further the objects of the " Servants' " Provident and Benevolent Society."

I conceive that this Society is founded upon a right principle, as it follows out the dictates of a correct appreciation of human nature, which requires every man, by personal exertion, and according to his own choice, to work out his own happiness; which prevents his valuing, nay, even his feeling satisfaction at, the prosperity which others have made for him. It is founded upon a right principle, because it endeavours to trace out a plan according to which, by providence, by present self-denial and perseverance, not only will the servant be raised in his physical and moral condition, but the master also will be taught how to direct his efforts in aiding the servant in his labour to secure to himself resources in cases of sickness, old age, and want of employment. It is founded on a right principle, because in its financial scheme there is no temptation held out to the servant by the prospect of possible extravagant advantages, which tend to transform his providence into a species of gambling; by convivial meetings, which lead him to ulterior expense; or by the privilege of balloting for the few prizes, which draws him into all the waste of time and excitement of an electioneering contest.

Such are the characteristics of several institutions, upon which servants and many of our other industrial classes place their reliance. And what can be more heartrending than to witness the breaking of banks, and the failure of such institutions, which not only mar the prospects of these unhappy people, and plunge them into sudden destitution, but destroy in others all confidence in the honesty or sagacity of those who preach to them the advantages of providence?

Let them well consider that, if they must embark in financial speculations, if they like to have convivial meetings, if they claim the right of governing the concerns of their own body, they must not risk for this, in one stake, their whole future existence, the whole prosperity of their families. Let them always bear in mind, that their savings are capital, that capital will only return a certain interest, and that any advantage offered beyond that interest has to be purchased at a commensurate risk of the capital itself.

The financial advantages which this Society holds out to servants rest upon the credit of the country at large, upon the faith of the Government, and are regulated by an Act of Parliament, called "the Deferred Annuities Act." They are shortly these: " According to published tables, " which I have before me, persons, whose fixed " income is below 150*l.* per annum, can, by small " instalments, purchase annuities deferred not less " than ten years, but beyond that limit to com- " mence at any period the depositor may name. " One annuity cannot be more than 30*l.*, but he " may purchase distinct annuities for his wife, or

" for his children on having attained to their
" fifteenth year. Should he at any time wish to
" withdraw his deposits before the annuity has
" commenced, they will be returned to him;
" should he die before that period, the deposits
" will be returned to the heirs. In such cases
" the only loss will be the interest upon the
" money deposited."

Although this wise and benevolent measure has been enacted so long ago as the third year of the reign of King William IV., I find, to my deep regret, that, during that whole time, only about 600 persons have availed themselves of its provisions. I can discover no other reason for this inadequate success, but that the existence of the Act is not generally known, or that people are afraid of law and Acts of Parliament, which they cannot understand on account of their complicated technical wording. I have heard another reason stated, to which, however, I give little credit, namely, that servants fear lest a knowledge that they are able to purchase annuities by savings from their wages might induce their masters to reduce them. I have a better opinion of the disposition of employers generally, and am convinced that, on the contrary, nothing counteracts more the liberality of masters than the idea, not wholly unfounded, that an increase of means, instead of prompting to saving, leads to extravagance.

It is one of the main objects of this meeting to draw public attention to this " Deferred Annuities " Act," and the main object of this Society is to form a medium by which servants may acquire the benefits proffered by it free from risk, cost, or trouble.

The other objects are : to provide a home for female servants out of place, the usefulness of which hardly requires a word of commendation ; to provide respectable lodgings for men-servants not lodged by their masters ; and to establish a Registry for domestic servants generally, which will form as well a place of advertisement for their services, as a record of their characters, from which they can be obtained upon application.

Any one who is acquainted with the annoyances and inconveniences connected with the present system of "characters to servants," will at once see the importance of the introduction of a system by which the servant will be protected from that ruin which the caprice of a single master (with whom he may even have lived for a short time only) may inflict upon him, and the master from the risk to which a character wrung from a former weak master, by the importunities of an undeserving servant, may expose him. Nor is it a small benefit to be conferred upon the servant, to enable him, by appealing to a long record of former services, to redeem the disqualification which a single fault might bring upon him.

Should we only succeed in inducing the public at large to consider all these points, we shall have the satisfaction of having furthered the interests of a class which we find recorded in the Report of the last Census as the most numerous in the British population.

I shall now call upon the Secretary to lay before you more in detail the points which I have slightly touched upon.

AT THE ENTERTAINMENT GIVEN BY

THE MERCHANT TAILORS' COMPANY.

[JUNE 11TH, 1849.]

GENTLEMEN,—

I THANK you sincerely for your expressions of kindness and cordiality towards me.

Although I have on former occasions met you in this room, it has always been for some charitable purpose, witnessing with delight the readiness with which this, and indeed all the great corporations of London, open the doors of their magnificent Halls at the call of charity. To-day I am here as a Brother Freeman of your Corporation, fulfilling a promise made from the time that you received me into your body. I am ashamed to own how long ago. I beg you not to measure, by the tardiness of my appearance, the value which I attach to the honour which you then conferred upon me, by electing me a Freeman of the Merchant Tailors' Company.

I remember well with what regret, when, shortly after I came of age, the Companies of the

Goldsmiths and of the Fishmongers offered me their freedom, I found myself compelled to decline this honour, being informed that, identified as they were by historical tradition, and still representing two opposite political parties, I could make a choice only of one of them, and, fully sensible that, like the Sovereign to whom I had just been united, and to devote my whole existence to whom it had become my privilege, I could belong only to the nation at large, free from the trammels and above the dissensions of political parties.

I well remember, too, how much pleased I was when the two Companies, waiving some of their statutes, finally agreed both to receive me amongst them; and my satisfaction is heightened when I consider that I owe to that decision the advantage of finding myself associated with you also.

Anybody may indeed feel proud to be enrolled a member of a Company which can boast of uninterrupted usefulness and beneficence during four centuries, and holds to this day the same honourable position in the estimation of the country which it did in the time of its first formation, although the progress of civilization and wealth has so vastly raised the community around it, exemplifying the possibility, in this happy country, of combining the general progress of mankind with a due reverence for the institutions, and even forms, which have been bequeathed to us by the piety and wisdom of our forefathers.

Let us join in the hope that this Corporation may continue in its charitable functions to be equally an object of respect to our children and children's children, and so drink " Prosperity to " the Merchant Tailors' Company."

ON PRESENTING COLOURS TO THE 23RD REGIMENT, ROYAL WELSH FUSILIERS.

[JULY 12TH, 1849.]

SOLDIERS OF THE ROYAL WELSH FUSILIERS,

THE ceremony which we are performing this day is a most important, and, to every soldier, a sacred one. It is the transmission to your care and keeping of the Colours which are henceforth to be borne before you, which will be the symbol of your honour, the rallying point in all moments of danger.

I feel most proud to be the person who is to transmit these Colours to a Regiment so renowned for its valour, fortitude, steadiness, and discipline.

In looking over the records of your services, I could not refrain from extracting a few, which show your deeds to have been intimately connected with all the great periods in our history. The Regiment was raised in 1688. Its existence therefore began with the settlement of the liberties of the country. It fought at the Boyne under Schomberg; captured Namur in Flanders in 1693; formed part of the great Marlborough's legions at Blenheim and Oudenarde; fought in 1742 at Dettingen and Fontenoy; decided the battle of Minden in 1751, for which the name of *Minden* is inscribed on the colours; showed examples of valour and perseverance in America in 1773, at Boston, Charlestown, Brandywine, and Edgehill; accompanied the Duke of York to Holland; was amongst the first to land in Egypt, under the brave Abercrombie, and, later, the last to embark at Corunna; but between these two important services fought at Copenhagen, and at the taking of Martinique. *Egypt, Martinique, and Corunna* are waving in these Colours. In the Peninsula the Regiment won for their Colours, under the Duke, the names of *Albuera, Badajoz, Salamanca, Vittoria, Pyrenees, Nivelles, Orthes, and Toulouse.* The deeds performed at Albuera are familiar to everybody who has read Napier's inimitable description of that action. The Regiment was victorious for the last time over a powerful enemy at the Duke's last great victory at Waterloo.

Although you were all of course well acquainted with these glorious records, I have thought it right to refer to them as a proof that they have not been forgotten by others, and as the best mode of appealing to you to show yourselves at all times worthy of the name you bear.

Take these Colours, one emphatically called the Queen's (let it be a pledge of your loyalty to your Sovereign, and of obedience to the laws of your country); the other, more especially the Regimental one, let that be a pledge of your determination to maintain the honour of your Regiment. In looking at the one, you will think of your Sovereign—in looking at the other, you will think of those who have fought, bled, and conquered before you.

AT THE BANQUET GIVEN BY

THE RIGHT HON. THE LORD MAYOR,

THOMAS FARNCOMBE,

TO HER MAJESTY'S MINISTERS,

FOREIGN AMBASSADORS,

ROYAL COMMISSIONERS OF THE EXHIBITION OF 1851,

AND THE

MAYORS OF ONE HUNDRED AND EIGHTY TOWNS,

AT THE MANSION HOUSE.

[MARCH 21st, 1850.]

My Lord Mayor,—

I AM sincerely grateful for the kindness with which you have proposed my health, and to you, gentlemen, for the cordiality with which you have received this proposal.

It must indeed be most gratifying to me to find that a suggestion which I had thrown out, as appearing to me of importance at this time, should have met with such universal concurrence and approbation; for this has proved to me that the view I took of the peculiar character and claims of the time we live in was in accordance with the feelings and opinions of the country.

Gentlemen—I conceive it to be the duty of every educated person closely to watch and study the time in which he lives, and, as far as in him lies, to add his humble mite of individual exertion to further the accomplishment of what he believes Providence to have ordained.

Nobody, however, who has paid any attention to the peculiar features of our present era, will doubt for a moment that we are living at a period of most wonderful transition, which tends rapidly to accomplish that great end, to which, indeed, all history points—*the realization of the unity of mankind*. Not a unity which breaks down the limits and levels the peculiar characteristics of the different nations of the earth, but rather a unity, the *result and product* of those very national varieties and antagonistic qualities.

The distances which separated the different nations and parts of the globe are rapidly vanishing before the achievements of modern invention, and we can traverse them with incredible ease; the languages of all nations are known, and their acquirement placed within the reach of everybody; thought is communicated with the rapidity, and even by the power, of lightning. On the other hand, the *great principle of division of labour*, which may be called the moving power of civilization, is being extended to all branches of science, industry, and art.

Whilst formerly the greatest mental energies strove at universal knowledge, and that knowledge was confined to the few, now they are directed on specialities, and in these, again, even to the minutest points; but the knowledge acquired becomes at once the property of the community at large; for, whilst formerly discovery was wrapped in secrecy, the publicity of the present day causes that no sooner is a discovery or invention made than it is already improved upon and surpassed by competing efforts. The products of all quarters of the globe are placed at our disposal, and we have only to choose which is the best and the cheapest for our purposes, and the powers of production are intrusted to the stimulus of *competition and capital*.

So man is approaching a more complete fulfilment of that great and sacred mission which he has to perform in this world. His reason being created after the image of God, he has to use it to discover the laws by which the Almighty governs His creation, and, by making these laws his standard of action, to conquer nature to his use; himself a divine instrument.

Science discovers these laws of power, motion, and transformation; industry applies them to the raw matter, which the earth yields us in abundance, but which becomes valuable only by knowledge. Art teaches us the immutable laws of beauty and symmetry, and gives to our productions forms in accordance to them.

Gentlemen—the Exhibition of 1851 is to give us a true test and a living picture of the point of development at which the whole of mankind has arrived in this great task, and a new starting-point from which all nations will be able to direct their further exertions.

I confidently hope that the first impression which the view of this vast collection will produce upon the spectator will be that of deep thankfulness to the Almighty for the blessings which He has bestowed upon us already here below; and the second, the conviction that they can only be realized in proportion to the help which we are prepared to render each other; therefore, only by peace, love, and ready assistance, not only between individuals, but between the nations of the earth.

This being *my* conviction, I must be highly gratified to see here assembled the magistrates of all the important towns of this realm, sinking all their local and possibly political differences, the representatives of the different political opinions of the country, and the representatives of the different Foreign Nations—to-day representing only *one interest!*

Gentlemen—my original plan had been to carry out this undertaking with the help of the Society of Arts of London, which had long and usefully laboured in this direction, and by the means of private capital and enterprise. You have wished it otherwise, and declared that it was a work which the British people as a whole ought to undertake. I at once yielded to your wishes, feeling that it proceeded from a patriotic, noble, and generous spirit. On *your* courage, perseverance, and liberality, the undertaking now entirely depends. I feel the strongest confidence in these qualities of the British people, and I am sure that they will repose confidence in themselves—confidence that they will honourably sustain the contest of emulation, and that they will nobly carry out their proffered hospitality to their foreign competitors.

We, Her Majesty's Commissioners, are quite

alive to the innumerable difficulties which we shall have to overcome in carrying out the scheme; but, having confidence in you and in our own zeal and perseverance, at least, we require only *your confidence in us* to make us contemplate the result without any apprehension.

AT THE LAYING OF THE FOUNDATION STONE

OF THE

NATIONAL GALLERY AT EDINBURGH.

[AUGUST 30TH, 1850.]

GENTLEMEN,—

NOW that this ceremony is concluded, you must allow me to express to you how much satisfaction it has given me to have had it in my power to comply with your invitation, and to lay the foundation stone of this important National institution, and that this should have coincided with the moment when Her Majesty the Queen has come among you, and has given you a further proof of her attachment to this country, by taking up her abode, if for a short time only, in the ancient palace of her ancestors in this capital, where she has been received with such unequivocal demonstrations of loyalty and affection.

The building, of which we have just begun the foundation, is a temple to be erected to the Fine Arts; the Fine Arts which have so important an influence upon the development of the mind and feeling of a people, and which are so generally taken as the type of the degree and character of that development, that it is on the fragments of works of art, come down to us from bygone nations, that we are wont to form our estimate of the state of their civilization, manners, customs, and religion.

Let us hope that the impulse given to the culture of the Fine Arts in this country, and the daily increasing attention bestowed upon it by the people at large, will not only tend to refine and elevate the national tastes, but will also lead to the production of works which, if left behind us as memorials of our age, will give to after generations an adequate idea of our advanced state of civilization.

It must be an additional source of gratification to me to find, that part of the funds rendered available for the support of this undertaking should be the ancient grant which, at the union of the two kingdoms, was secured towards the encouragement of the fisheries and manufactures of Scotland, as it affords a most pleasing proof that those important branches of industry have arrived at that stage of manhood and prosperity when, no longer requiring the aid of a fostering

Government, they can maintain themselves independently, relying upon their own vigour and activity, and can now in their turn lend assistance and support to their younger and weaker sisters, the Fine Arts.

Gentlemen, the history of this grant exhibits to us the picture of a most healthy national progress: the ruder arts connected with the necessaries of life *first* gaining strength; then education and science supervening and directing further exertions; and lastly, the arts which only adorn life becoming longed for by a prosperous and educated people.

May nothing disturb this progress, and may, by God's blessing, that peace and prosperity be preserved to the nation, which will insure to it a long continuance of moral and intellectual enjoyment!

AT THE BANQUET GIVEN BY
THE LORD MAYOR OF YORK,
AND THE MAYORS OF THE CHIEF CITIES AND TOWNS OF THE UNITED KINGDOM,
TO THE LORD MAYOR OF LONDON.

[OCTOBER 25TH, 1850.]

My Lord Mayor,—

I AM very sensible of your kindness in proposing my health, and I beg you, gentlemen, to believe that I feel very deeply your demonstrations of good will and cordiality towards myself. I can assure you that I fully reciprocate these sentiments, and that it has given me sincere pleasure to meet you, the representatives of all the important towns of the kingdom, again assembled at a festive board, in token of the unity and harmony of feeling which prevails amongst those whom you represent, and on which, I am persuaded, the happiness and well-being of the country so materially depends.

It was an idea honourable at once to the liberality and the discernment of the Lord

Mayor of London to invite you to assemble under his hospitable roof before you started in the important undertaking upon which you were going to enter; and when, according to ancient custom, the loving-cup went round, it was a pledge you gave each other, that, whatever the rivalries of your different localities might be, you would, in the approaching contest, all act and appear *as one*, representing your country at the gathering of the products of the nations of the earth.

I see by your anxiety to return, before your terms of office shall have expired, the compliment which London has paid you, that you personally appreciate, to its full extent, the intention of its chief magistrate ; and you could not have selected a better place for your meeting than this venerable city, which is so much connected with the recollections and the history of the empire, and is now pre-eminent as the centre of a district in which a high state of agriculture is blended with a most extensive production of manufactures.

But I see, likewise, in your anxiety to meet us, Her Majesty's Commissioners, again, a proof of your earnest and continued zeal in the cause of the approaching Exhibition. It could not be by the impetus of a momentary enthusiasm, but only by a steady perseverance and sustained effort, that you could hope to carry out your great undertaking, and ensure for yourselves and the nation an honourable position in the comparison which you have invited.

If, to cheer you on in your labours, by no means terminated, you should require an assurance that that spirit of activity and perseverance *is* abroad in the country, I can give you that assurance on the ground of the information which reaches us from all quarters, and I can add to it our personal conviction, that the works in preparation will be such as to dispel any apprehension for the position which British industry will maintain.

From abroad, also, all the accounts which we receive lead us to expect that the works which are to be sent will be numerous and of a superior character.

Although we perceive, in some countries, a fear that the advantages to be derived from the Exhibition will be mainly reaped by England, and a consequent distrust in the effects of our scheme upon their own interests, we must at the same time freely and gratefully acknowledge that our invitation has been received by all nations, with whom communication was possible, in that spirit of liberality and friendship in which it was tendered, and that they are making great exertions and incurring great expenses in order to meet our plans.

Of our own doings at the Commission I should have preferred to remain silent; but I cannot let this opportunity pass without telling you how much benefit we have derived, in our difficult labours, from your uninterrupted confidence in the intentions, at least, which guided our decisions, and that there has been no difference of opinion on any one subject, between us and the different local Committees, which has not, upon personal consultation, and after open explanation and discussion, vanished, and given way to agreement and identity of purpose.

There is but one alloy to my feelings of satisfaction and pleasure in seeing you here assembled again, and that is, the painful remembrance that one is missing from amongst us who felt so warm an interest in our scheme and took so active a part in promoting its success, the last act of whose public life was attending at the Royal Commission; my admiration for whose talents and character, and gratitude for whose devotion to the Queen, and private friendship towards myself, I feel a consolation in having this public opportunity to express.

Only at our last meeting we were still admiring his eloquence and the earnestness with which he appealed to you to uphold, by your exertions and personal sacrifices, what was to him the highest object—the honour of his country; he met you the following day, together with other Commissioners, to confer with you upon the details of our undertaking; and you must have been struck, as everybody has been who has had the benefit of his advice upon practical points, with the attention, care, and sagacity with which he treated the minutest details, proving that to a great mind nothing is little, from the knowledge that in the moral and intellectual, as in the physical world, the smallest point is only a link in that great chain, and holds its appointed place in that great whole, which is governed by the Divine Wisdom.

The constitution of Sir Robert Peel's mind was peculiarly that of a statesman, and of an English statesman: he was liberal from feeling, but conservative upon principle. Whilst his impulse drove him to foster progress, his sagacious mind and great experience showed him how easily the whole machinery of a state and of society is deranged, and how important, but how difficult also, it is to direct its further development in accordance with its fundamental principles, like organic growth in nature. It was peculiar to him, that in great things, as in small, all the difficulties and objections occurred to him first; he would anxiously consider them, pause, and warn against rash resolutions; but having convinced himself, after a long and careful investigation, that a step was not only right to be taken, but of the practical mode also of safely taking it, it became to him a necessity and a duty to take it: all his caution and apparent timidity changed into courage and power of action, and at the same time readiness cheerfully to make any personal sacrifice which its execution might demand.

Gentlemen, if he has had so great an influence over this country, it was from the nation recognizing in his qualities the true type of the English character, which is essentially practical. Warmly attached to his institutions, and revering the bequests left to him by the industry, wisdom, and piety of his forefathers, the Englishman attaches little value to any theoretical scheme. It will attract his attention only after having been for some time placed before him; it must have been thoroughly investigated and discussed before he will entertain it. Should it be an empty theory, it will fall to the ground during this time of probation; should it survive this trial, it will be on account of the practical qualities contained in it; but its adoption in the end will entirely depend upon its harmonizing with the national feeling, the historic development of the country, and the peculiar nature of its institutions.

It is owing to these national qualities that England, whilst constantly progressing, has still preserved the integrity of her constitution from the earliest times, and has been protected from wild schemes whose chief charm lies in their novelty, whilst around us we have seen unfortunately whole nations distracted, and the very fabric of society endangered, from the levity with which the result of the experience of generations, the growth of ages, has been thrown away to give place to temporarily favourite ideas.

Taking this view of the character of our country, I was pleased when I saw the plan of the Exhibition of 1851 undergo its ordeal of doubt, discussion, and even opposition; and I hope that I may now gather from the energy and earnestness with which its execution is pursued, that the nation is convinced that it accords with its interests and the position which England has taken in the world.

AT THE DINNER OF THE ROYAL ACADEMY.

[MAY 3RD, 1851.]

Mr. President,

My Lords and Gentlemen,—

You have been very kind in responding with so much warmth to the toast which your President has just proposed to you, and he will allow me to thank him very cordially for the flattering expressions which he used towards myself in introducing to you that toast.

I shall feel very happy if the future should prove that the Great Exhibition, to which all nations have so generously contributed, should, amongst other advantages which I firmly hope will result from it, likewise tend to assist in the promotion of the Fine Arts in this country, of which you are the representatives; and I feel proud that we can show to the many foreigners who are now visiting our shores specimens of British art such as these walls display.

Although I have, since my first arrival in this country, never once missed visiting the Exhibition of the Royal Academy, and have always derived the greatest pleasure and instruction from these visits, it is but seldom that my engagements will allow me to join in your festive dinner. I have, however, upon this occasion, made it a point to do so, in order to assist in what may be considered the inauguration festival of your newly-elected President, at whose election I have heartily rejoiced, not only on account of my high estimate of his qualities, but also on account of my feelings of regard towards him personally.

It would be presumptuous in me to speak to you of his talent as an artist, for that is well known to you, and of it you are the best judges; or of his merits as an author, for you are all familiar with his works, or at least ought to be so; or of his amiable character as a man, for that also you must have had opportunities to estimate: but my connection with him, now for nine years, on Her Majesty's Commission of the Fine Arts, has enabled me to know what you can know less, and what is of the greatest value in a President of the Royal Academy—I mean that kindness of heart and refinement of feeling which guided him in all his communications, often most difficult and delicate, with the different artists whom we had to invite to competition, whose works we had to criticise, whom we had to employ or to reject.

Gentlemen, the production of all works in art or poetry requires, in their conception and execution, not only an exercise of the intellect, skill, and patience, but particularly *a concurrent warmth of feeling* and a free flow of imagination. This renders them most tender plants, which will thrive only in an atmosphere calculated to maintain that warmth, and that atmosphere is one of *kindness*—kindness towards the artist personally as well as towards his production. An unkind word of criticism passes like a cold blast over their tender shoots, and shrivels them up, checking the flow of the sap, which was rising to produce, perhaps, multitudes of flowers and fruit. But still criticism is absolutely necessary to the development of art, and the injudicious praise of an inferior work becomes an insult to superior genius.

In this respect our times are peculiarly unfavourable when compared with those when Madonnas were painted in the seclusion of convents; for we have now on the one hand the eager competition of a vast array of artists of every degree of talent and skill, and on the other, as judge, a great public, for the greater part wholly uneducated in art, and thus led by professional writers, who often strive to impress the public with a great idea of their own artistic knowledge by the merciless manner in which they treat works which cost those who produced them the highest efforts of mind or feeling.

The works of art, by being publicly exhibited and offered for sale, are becoming articles of trade, following as such the unreasoning laws of markets and fashion; and public and even private patronage is swayed by their tyrannical influence.

It is, then, to an institution like this, gentlemen, that we must look for a counterpoise to these evils. Here young artists are educated and taught the mysteries of their profession; those who have distinguished themselves, and given proof of their talent and power, receive a badge of acknowledgment from their professional brethren by being elected Associates of the Academy; and are at last, after long toil and continued exertion, received into a select aristocracy of a limited number, and shielded in any further struggle by their well-established reputation, of which the letters R.A. attached to their names give a pledge to the public.

If this body is often assailed from without, it shares only the fate of every aristocracy; if more than another, this only proves that it is even more difficult to sustain an aristocracy of merit than one of birth or of wealth, and may serve as a useful check upon yourselves when tempted at your elections to let personal predilection compete with real merit.

Of one thing, however, you may rest assured, and that is the continued favour of the Crown. The same feelings which actuated George the Third in founding this institution, still actuate the Crown in continuing to it its patronage and support, recognizing in you a constitutional link, as it were, between the Crown itself and the artistic body. And when I look at the assemblage of guests at this table, I may infer that the Crown does not stand alone in this respect, but that its feelings are shared also by the great and noble in the land.

May the Academy long flourish, and continue its career of usefulness!

AT THE THIRD JUBILEE OF

THE INCORPORATED SOCIETY

FOR THE

PROPAGATION OF THE GOSPEL IN FOREIGN PARTS.

[JUNE 16TH, 1851.]

MY LORDS, LADIES, AND GENTLEMEN,—

WE are assembled here to-day in order to celebrate the third jubilee of the foundation of the "Society for the Propagation of the "Gospel in Foreign Parts," incorporated by Royal Charter, and one of the chief sources of the spiritual aid which the Church of England affords to our extensive colonial dependencies.

We are not commemorating, however, an isolated fact which may have been glorious or useful to the country, but we are thankfully acknowledging the Divine favour which has attended exertions which have been unremitting during the lapse of one hundred and fifty years. We are met at the same time to invoke the further continuance of that favour, pledging ourselves not to relax in our efforts to extend to those of our brethren who are settled in distant lands, and building up communities and states where man's footsteps had first to be imprinted on the soil, and wild nature yet to be conquered to his use, those blessings of Christianity which form the foundation of our community and of our state.

This Society was first chartered by that great man William the Third, the greatest sovereign this country has to boast of; by whose sagacity and energy was closed that bloody struggle for civil and religious liberty which so long had convulsed this country, and who secured to us the inestimable advantages of our constitution and of our Protestant faith.

Having thus placed the country upon a safe basis at home, he could boldly meet her foes abroad, and contribute to the foundation of that colonial empire which forms so important a part of our present greatness; and honour be to him for his endeavour to place this foundation upon the rock of the Church.

The first jubilee of the Society fell in times when religious apathy had succeeded to the over-excitement of the preceding age. Lax morals and a sceptical philosophy began to undermine the Christian faith, treating with indifference and even ridicule the most sacred objects. Still this Society persevered in its labours with unremitting zeal, turning its chief attention to the North American continent, where a young and vigorous society was rapidly growing into a people.

The second jubilee found this country in a most critical position: she had obtained, by the peace of Amiens, a moment's respite from the tremendous contest in which she had been engaged with her continental rival, and which she had soon to renew, in order to maintain her own existence, and to secure a permanent peace to Europe. Since the last jubilee, the American colonies, which had originally been peopled chiefly by British subjects who had left their homes to escape the yoke of religious intolerance and oppression, had thrown off their allegiance to the mother country in defence of civil rights, the attachment to which they had carried with them from the British soil. Yet this Society was not dismayed, but in a truly Christian spirit continued its labours in the neighbouring North American and West Indian settlements.

This, the third jubilee, falls in a happier epoch, when peace is established in Europe, and religious fervour is rekindled, and at an auspicious moment when we are celebrating a festival of the civilization of mankind, to which all quarters of the globe have contributed their productions, and are sending their people, for the first time recognizing their advancement as a common good, their interests as identical, their mission on earth the same.

And this civilization rests on Christianity, could only be raised on Christianity, can only be maintained by Christianity! the blessings of which are now carried by this Society to the vast territories of India and Australasia, which last are again to be peopled by the Anglo-Saxon race.

Whilst we have thus to congratulate ourselves upon our state of temporal prosperity, harmony at home, and peace abroad, we cannot help deploring that the Church, whose exertions for the progress of Christianity and civilization we are to-day acknowledging, should be afflicted by internal dissensions and attacks from without. I have no fear, however, for her safety and ultimate welfare so long as she holds fast to what our ancestors gained for us at the Reformation—*the Gospel and the unfettered right of its use.*

The dissensions and difficulties which we witness in this as in every other Church arise from the natural and necessary conflict of the two antagonistic principles which move human society in Church as well as in State; I mean the principles of *individual liberty and of allegiance and submission to the will of the community*, exacted by it for its own preservation.

These conflicting principles cannot safely be disregarded: they must be reconciled. To this country belongs the honour of having succeeded in this mighty task, as far as the State is concerned, whilst other nations are still wrestling with it; and I feel persuaded that the same earnest zeal and practical wisdom which has made her political Constitution an object of admiration to other nations will, under God's blessing, make her Church likewise a model to the world.

Let us look upon this assembly as a token of future hope; and may the harmony which reigns amongst us at this moment, and which we owe to having met in furtherance of a common holy object, be by the Almighty permanently bestowed upon the Church.

AT THE
ROYAL AGRICULTURAL SOCIETY'S SHOW.

[WINDSOR, JULY 16TH, 1851.]

My Lord Duke,
My Lords and Gentlemen,—

I AM very sensible of the honour which you have done me in proposing my health; and I can assure you, gentlemen, that the kind way in which you have responded to the toast will never be forgotten by me.

Some years have elapsed already since I last dined with you in this migratory pavilion, and I am glad that you should have pitched it this day under the walls of Windsor Castle, and that I should myself have an opportunity of bidding you a hearty welcome in the Home Park.

Your encampment singularly contrasts with that which the barons of England, the feudal lords of the land, with their retainers, erected round old Windsor Castle on a similar mead, though not exactly in the same locality. They came then clad in steel, with lance and war-horse;

you appear in a more peaceful attire, and the animals you bring with you are the tokens of your successful cultivation of the arts of peace. King John came trembling amongst his subjects, unwillingly compelled to sign that Great Charter which has ever since been your birthright. Your Sovereign came confiding among her loyal and loving people; she came to admire the results of their industry, and to encourage them to persevere in their exertions.

And the gratification which the Queen has felt at the sight of your splendid collection must, I am sure, be participated in by all who examine it. I am doubly pleased at this success, not only because it is witnessed by the many visitors from foreign lands now within our shores, whom every Englishman must wish to inspire with respect for the state of British agriculture, but also because I feel to a certain degree personally responsible for having deprived you of one generally most interesting feature of your show: I mean the field-fruits and the agricultural machines and implements. Though separated from your collection, they are seen to great advantage in another Royal Park; and you will have been glad to hear that, "whatever the diffi-
" culty may be in deciding upon the superiority

" of the works of industry and art sent to the
" Crystal Palace by the different nations of the
" earth, the British agricultural implements are
" acknowledged by common consent to stand
" there almost without a rival."

Let me now use the privilege which your President has allowed me to enjoy, in proposing to you, as a toast, " Prosperity to the Royal Agri-
" cultural Society." To its exhibitions, the means of comparison which they have afforded, and the emulation which they have stimulated, we owe to a great extent the progress which British agriculture has made of late. To this Society belongs the honour to have been one of the first to appreciate the value of such exhibitions, and to have from the beginning liberally and fearlessly admitted all competitors without restriction.

I drink, " Prosperity to the Royal Agricul-
" tural Society."

AT THE

BANQUET AT THE TRINITY HOUSE.

[JUNE 4TH, 1853.]

1.

WHEREVER Englishmen meet at a public dinner they make it their pride to take no proceedings without first drinking to the health of "The Queen." The Corporation of the Trinity House yield in feelings of loyalty to none of Her Majesty's subjects.—Gentlemen!

"THE QUEEN!"

2.

The toast I have now to propose to you is that of the Royal Family.

It is a blessing attending the monarchical institutions of this country, that the domestic relations and the domestic happiness of the sovereign are inseparable from the relations and happiness of the people at large. In the progress of the Royal Family through life is reflected, as it were, the progress of the generation to which they belong, and out of the common sympathy felt for them arises an additional bond of union amongst the people themselves. I have often been deeply touched by the many proofs of kindness, and, I may say, almost parental affection, with which the Prince of Wales and the rest of our young family have been welcomed on their earliest appearance. May God grant that they may some day repay that affection, and make themselves worthy of it by fulfilling the expectations which the country so fondly cherishes!

3.

I am sure that you could not have entered this room without feeling a pang at missing from the chair, which I am this day called upon to occupy, that great man whose loss we still find it almost impossible to realise. It would be repugnant to our feelings to take another step in the proceedings of this evening without paying a mournful tribute to his name. Let us drink in solemn silence to the memory of the great Duke, to whom this Corporation, as well as the whole nation, are so deeply indebted.

4.

I have now to invite you to drink to the British Army and Navy, and in doing so I would add to the toast the names of the two distinguished men who preside over them, the General Commanding-in-Chief and the First Lord of the Admiralty, Viscount Hardinge and Sir James Graham.

It is under the protection of these two great services that this country has attained an extent of power, wealth, and territory, without a parallel in history.

We are rich, prosperous, and contented, therefore peaceful by instinct.

We are becoming, I hope, daily more civilized and religious, and, therefore, daily recognizing more and more, that the highest use to which we can apply the advantages with which an all-bountiful Providence has favoured us, is to extend and maintain the blessings of Peace. I hope, however, the day may never arrive which would find us either so enervated by the enjoyment of riches and luxury, or so sunk in the decrepitude of age, that, from a miserable eagerness to cling to our mere wealth and comforts, we should be deaf to the calls of Honour and Duty.

5.

The Health of Her Majesty's Ministers is the toast which I now ask you to drink.

The Brethren of the Trinity House have at all times been anxious cordially to co-operate with Her Majesty's Government, by whomsoever conducted; they know no politics, but feel that the responsibility which is imposed upon those men who are intrusted with the care of the multifarious interests of this vast empire is an awful one, requiring every assistance which it may be in the power of individuals or public bodies to afford. They are convinced also, that, however party violence may separate public men from each other, they are all equally influenced by one sole consideration, the good of their country.

The Earl of Aberdeen and Her Majesty's Ministers.

6.

I am very grateful to you, gentlemen, for the kindness with which you have received the toast proposed by the Deputy Master, and beg to thank him for the obliging terms in which he has proposed my health.

When this important Corporation elected me as their Master, I was well aware that I did not owe this to any personal merit of my own, giving me a claim to such an honour, and I might well have paused before I undertook to succeed, in any task or position, that great Man whom few can hope to equal in talent, energy, and wisdom; but I saw in the choice of the Brethren a desire to mark their attachment to the Throne, and, in my own acceptance, a means for the Queen to testify through me her interest and solicitude for British Commerce and Shipping, and for the British Seaman. This Corporation has had, since King Henry the Eighth, one of the high functions of administration delegated to it by the State, that, namely, of lighting the coast, piloting vessels, and tendering aid and assistance to the merchant seaman worn out by the toils and the privations of his adventurous life. The world bears testimony to the manner in which this duty has been discharged; and I can refer to none which can be more satisfactory to the Corporation than that which has been only recently borne by our brethren on the other side of the Atlantic.

Gentlemen! The ever-changing, renovating, and preserving influences of time have, in their inevitable operation, made themselves felt also with regard to this Institution, and the greatest credit is due to the wisdom and patriotism of the Brethren for having rightly judged and appreciated the demands made by them. Having hitherto enjoyed the almost irresponsible power of taxing the public for the objects of their trust, they cheerfully consented to submit their affairs to the utmost publicity, as well as to a control from Government. Their own power they surrendered without a murmur; the interests of the poor seaman they thought themselves bound to advocate. Whilst repudiating any wish to retain patronage in the distribution of alms, which in fact they had hitherto looked upon rather as an anxious and responsible duty, they exerted themselves to the utmost to bring the claims of this deserving class before the Government; and whatever may be the inherent difficulty in framing a measure, the purport of which is to relieve a *class*, without impairing its moral strength and self-dependence, they still hope that the Legislature will not shrink from the attempt.

Gentlemen—for all the Trinity House may have done, thanks are solely due to the excellent Deputy Master, and the Elder Brethren by whom he is so efficiently supported. Let us drink his health, and Prosperity to the Corporation of the Trinity House.

7.

One of the peculiar features of the public life of this country is, that no public body stands isolated in the community, but that it endeavours to establish and maintain an organic connection with the other interests and classes of society, securing thereby the inestimable advantage of harmony of action and feeling. The Corporation of the Trinity House has sought to effect this through its Honorary Brethren; and I have only to point to those who now sit as such round this table to prove that, whilst the Corporation has been guided in its choice solely by the desire to connect itself with the men who stand highest in the estimation of their country, the most distinguished men have, on their side, deemed it an honour to become the objects of that choice.

In drinking to the Honorary Brethren, I would mention the name of the gallant Admiral of the Fleet, Sir Byam Martin, who may be truly called the Father of his profession.

AT THE BICENTENARY FESTIVAL OF THE CORPORATION OF THE SONS OF THE CLERGY.

[MAY 10TH, 1854.]

My Lord Mayor,—

ALLOW me to return you, on my own behalf, and on that of the Royal Family, my best thanks for the manner in which you have proposed our health, and to you, gentlemen, for the cordial response which you have made to the toast.

I am, indeed, highly gratified to have been a witness to the *Two Hundredth Anniversary* of this Festival, testifying, as it does, that the people of this country do not relax in efforts which they have once undertaken, and do not forsake the spirit which animated their forefathers.

When our ancestors purified the Christian faith, and shook off the yoke of a domineering Priesthood, they felt that the key-stone of that wonderful fabric which had grown up in the dark times of the middle ages was the *Celibacy of the Clergy*, and shrewdly foresaw that their reformed faith and newly-won religious liberty would, on the contrary, only be secure in the hands of a clergy united with the people by every sympathy, national, personal, and domestic.

Gentlemen—this nation has enjoyed for three hundred years the blessing of a Church Establishment which rests upon this basis, and cannot be too grateful for the advantages afforded by the fact that the Christian Ministers not only preach the *doctrines* of Christianity, but live among their congregations an example for the discharge of every *Christian duty*, as husbands, fathers, and masters of families, themselves capable of fathoming the whole depth of human feelings, desires, and difficulties.

Whilst we must gratefully acknowledge that they have, as a body, worthily fulfilled this high and difficult task, we must bear in mind that we deny them an equal participation in one of the actuating motives of life—the one which, amongst the "children of this generation," exercises, perhaps of necessity, the strongest influence—I mean the desire for the acquisition and accumulation of the goods of this world.

Gentlemen—the appellation of a "money-

"making parson" is not only a reproach but a condemnation for a clergyman, depriving him at once of all influence over his congregation. Yet this man, who has to shun opportunities for acquiring wealth open to most of us, and who has himself only an often scanty life-income allotted to him for his services, has a wife and children like ourselves; and we wish him to have the same solicitude for their welfare which we feel for our own.

Are we not bound, then, to do what we can to relieve his mind from anxiety, and to preserve his children from destitution, when it shall have pleased the Almighty to remove him from the scene of his labours?

You have given an answer in the affirmative by your presence here to-day; and although this institution can do *materially* but little, morally it gives a public recognition of the claims which the sons of the clergy have upon the sympathy and liberality of the community at large, and as such is of the greatest value.

May it continue for further hundreds of years as a band of union between Clergy and Laity, and on each recurring centenary may it find this nation ever advancing in prosperity, civilization, and piety!

DINNER AT THE TRINITY HOUSE.

[JUNE 21st, 1854.]

1.

"THE QUEEN."

2.

THE toast which I have to propose to you is that of—

"His Royal Highness the PRINCE OF WALES
" and the rest of the ROYAL FAMILY."

In doing so, I am impelled to refer to one Member of that family who is at present engaged in the discharge of arduous duties in the East. He is the only one whom both his position and his age permitted to offer his services on this occasion, and I rejoice at his having done so, as a proof that the Members of the Royal Family are at all times ready to serve—ay! and, if necessary, to bleed for their country.

3.

"The Army and Navy."

The toast which I have now to propose to you —" The Army and Navy of Great Britain "— will be drunk by you with peculiar emotions at this time, as your eyes are turned towards these Services, your hearts beat for them, and with their success the welfare and the honour of the country are so intimately bound up.

They will do their duty as they have always done, and may the Almighty bless their efforts!

What is asked to be achieved by them in this instance is a task of inordinate difficulty, not only from the nature and climate of the country in which they are fighting, but also from the peculiarity of the enemy to whom they are opposed, as it may so happen that the Army may meet a foe of ten times its number, whilst the Fleet may find it impossible to meet one at all.

All these difficulties, however, may be considered as compensated by the goodness of our cause, " the vindication of the public law of " Europe," and the fact that we have fighting by our side a Power, the military prowess and vigour of which we have hitherto chiefly known from the severity of long and anxious contests.

If there be a contest between us now, it will be one of emulation, and not of enmity.

" The Army and Navy of Great Britain, and
" the Health of the Right Honourable Lord
" Viscount Hardinge, and the Right Honour-
" able Sir James Graham, Bart."

4.

We are honoured to-day by the presence of the Members of Her Majesty's Government. The only return which the country can make to those men, who sacrifice their own quiet, privacy, and often health, to the arduous and anxious labours of conducting the public business, is an acknowledgment of the sincerity and disinterestedness of their motives of action. This it is which I invite you to give upon the present occasion in drinking the health of Her Majesty's Government, and Lord John Russell, Lord President of the Council.

6.

I am very much obliged to you for the kind expressions in which you have proposed my health, and to the company for the way in which they have received it. But I have to thank you, the Elder Brethren, especially, for the mark of confidence which you have shown me in reelecting me as your Master, a confidence which I assure you that I appreciate highly, and of which I shall be anxious to prove myself at all times worthy. Although the duties of my office are hardly more than nominal, I attach the greatest value to my personal connection with your Corporation — the only public body to whom duties are intrusted so deeply affecting the interests of the commerce, the shipping, and the seamen of this country. I must also take this opportunity to congratulate you on the working of the important alterations made last year in your constitution, as they have proved a successful attempt at that difficult and nice operation, to bring the spontaneous activity of a public body into harmony with the general feelings of the country, as represented in its Government, without destroying all individual and organic life by the killing influence of an arbitrary mechanical centralization.

In proposing to you to drink to the future prosperity of the Corporation, I shall but follow your wishes in coupling the toast with the name of the Deputy-Master, to whose zeal and ability so much of its present prosperity is due.

7.

I have the honour of naming to you, as the next toast, "The Honorary Brethren of the "Corporation." They are composed of men, although varying in their political opinions, yet all standing high in the estimation of their country—an esteem which they have earned by distinguished services rendered to the State, and the Corporation is justly proud of its connection with them. I would ask permission to couple the toast with the name of The Earl of Haddington.

14.

In returning the thanks of the Corporation to our distinguished guests, I beg leave to propose to you "The Health of the Lord High Chan-
" cellor of England, and the other noble and
" distinguished persons who have this day
" honoured the Corporation by their presence."

SPEECHES DELIVERED AT THE

ANNUAL DINNER AT THE TRINITY-HOUSE.

[JUNE 9TH, 1855.]

1.
"THE QUEEN!"

2.

I PROPOSE to you the health of the PRINCE of WALES and the rest of the ROYAL FAMILY. May they prosper under the favour of the Almighty!

3.

The toast which I now propose to you—the "Army and Navy"—is one in which I am sure no Englishman can join at this moment without the feelings of the deepest emotion. In their keeping stand the honour and the best interests of this country—I may say the interests of the civilization of Europe. And nobly have they done their duty! whether in the daring impetuosity of attack, in the cool intrepidity of defence, or the noble and truly Christian patience with which they have endured nameless sufferings and privations! They have set us all an example well worthy of imitation, and making us proud of the generation to which we belong. May God grant that their exertions may be crowned with the success they have striven to deserve, and that they may, by the side of our noble and gallant allies, conquer to the world a peace which may secure its tranquillity and prosperity from any further interruption!

I drink "The health of Viscount Hardinge, "Sir Charles Wood, and the Army and Navy. "Success to their exertions!"

4.

I now propose to you the health of "Her Ma- "jesty's Ministers."

If there ever was a time when the Queen's Government, by whomsoever conducted, required the support—ay, not the support alone, but the confidence, goodwill, and sympathy of their fellow countrymen, it is the present. It is not the way to success in war to support it, however ardently and energetically, and to run down and weaken those who have to conduct it. We are engaged with a mighty adversary, who uses against us all those wonderful powers which have sprung up under the generating influence of our liberty and our civilization, and employs them with all the force which unity of purpose and action, impenetrable secresy, and uncontrolled despotic power give him; whilst we have to meet him under a state of things intended for peace and the promotion of that very civilization—a civilization the offspring of public discussion, the friction of parties, and popular control over the government of the State. The Queen has no power to levy troops, and none at her command, except such as voluntarily offer their services. Her Government can entertain no measures for the prosecution of the war without having to explain them publicly in Parliament; her armies and fleets can make no movement, nor even prepare for any, without its being proclaimed by the press; and no mistake, however trifling, can occur, no weakness exist, which it may be of the utmost importance to conceal from the world, without its being publicly denounced, and even frequently exaggerated, with a morbid satisfaction. The Queen's ambassadors can carry on no negociation which has not to be publicly defended by entering into all the arguments which a negociator, to have success, must be able to shut up in the innermost recesses of his heart—nay, at the most critical moment, when the complication of military measures and diplomatic negociations may be at their height, an adverse vote in Parliament may of a sudden deprive her of all her confidential servants.

Gentlemen! Constitutional Government is under a heavy trial, and can only pass triumphantly through it, if the country will grant its confidence—a patriotic, indulgent, and self-denying confidence—to Her Majesty's Government. Without this, all their labours must be in vain.

I hope you will drink with me "The Health " of Viscount Palmerston and Her Majesty's " Ministers."

5.

I am much obliged to you for your kindness in proposing my health, and to the company for the reception which they have given to the toast.

It always affords me great satisfaction to be able to preside at your annual Dinner, particularly when I can congratulate you on the completion of another year of usefulness and of successful labour. This I am enabled to do on the present occasion, and have only to point to the satisfactory working of your extended jurisdiction over the Cinque Port pilots—to the progress of your lighthouses—to the success in your efforts to ameliorate the condition of the ballast-heavers—and to the fact that you have, through the Board of Trade, entered into a communication with Her Majesty's Colonies, for the purpose of laying down a complete system of lighting, based on your knowledge and experience, in those important but remotely-removed parts of the world.

It is to the indefatigable zeal of the Deputy-Master that much of this success is due; you will, therefore, I doubt not, gladly join with me in drinking to *his good health*, in connection with the toast of the evening—" Prosperity to " the Corporation of the Trinity House."

AT THE OPENING OF

THE NEW CATTLE MARKET,

IN COPENHAGEN FIELDS, ISLINGTON.

[JUNE 13TH, 1855.]

MY LORD MAYOR AND GENTLEMEN,—

ACCEPT the expression of my hearty thanks for your kind welcome, and for the gratifying assurance of your loyal and affectionate attachment to the Queen and her Family. I have been much pleased by the opportunity which your kind invitation has afforded me of seeing and admiring the great work which you this day open to the public—a work which not only deserves all admiration in itself, on account of the excellence of the arrangements and the magnificence of the design, but which will, I trust, be found eminently conducive to the comfort and health of the City of London. That its success will be commensurate with the spirit in which it has been undertaken and carried out I cannot doubt. A certain dislocation of habits and interests must inevitably attend the removal of the great City market from the site it has occupied for so many centuries, and this may possibly retard for the moment the fullest development of the undertaking; but any opposition arising from such causes will soon cease, and the farmers will, doubtless, soon learn to appreciate the boon thus conferred upon them by the Corporation of London in the increased facility which will be afforded to them for the transaction of their business and the comparative security with which they will be enabled to bring up and display their valuable stock in the Great Metropolitan Cattle Market.

[The LORD MAYOR gave the health of HIS ROYAL HIGHNESS, who, in responding to the toast, said]—

MY LORD MAYOR,—

I RETURN you my best thanks for the honour you have done me in proposing my health, and to you, gentlemen, for the kindness with which you have responded to the toast.

It has given me very great pleasure to have been able to accept the invitation of the Lord Mayor to be present at the opening of this splendid and useful work; and I beg to assure him that the oftener he shall invite me to similar ceremonies, the better I shall be pleased.

This wonderful metropolis, which has already gathered beneath its roofs nearly two million and a half of human beings, and has even within these last six years added not less than 290 miles of street to its extent, imperatively requires that those establishments which are to minister to the common wants of the whole should keep pace with its growth and magnitude. They can only be undertaken by public bodies, they can only be successfully carried out by public spirit. I know that the difficulties which have to be overcome, where so much private capital has acquired vested interests, are immense; but I hail the spirit which is rising amongst us, and which, I doubt not, will meet those difficulties. I hail this instance as an earnest of your determination to accept the duties which your position has imposed upon you, and as a proof that success will at all times reward a bold and conscientious execution of them.

I beg now to propose to you to drink the "Health of the Lord Mayor and Corporation of "the City of London, and Prosperity to the New "Metropolitan Cattle Market."

AT THE BANQUET IN

THE BIRMINGHAM TOWN HALL,

ON THE OCCASION OF LAYING THE FIRST STONE

OF THE

BIRMINGHAM AND MIDLAND INSTITUTE.

[NOVEMBER 22ND, 1855.]

[An Address having been presented by the Corporation, His Royal Highness in reply said—]

MR. MAYOR AND GENTLEMEN,—

THE cordial reception I have met with from you demands my warmest acknowledgments. You only, I assure you, do me justice in giving me credit for a deep interest in whatever may tend to promote the advancement of either the moral or the material good of the people of this country; but you are doing so in too flattering a manner, and attach too high a value to any service that it may have been in my power to render in this cause. I feel it would be a high privilege to be associated in any way with those who are making such noble efforts — and nowhere with more energy and perseverance than in Birmingham — for the improvement of their fellow-countrymen; and to be allowed to witness the success of those efforts will be a more than sufficient reward for any assistance I may myself have been enabled to afford.

[Lord CALTHORPE having read the Address of the Council of the Institute,

HIS ROYAL HIGHNESS said—]

MY LORDS AND GENTLEMEN,—

I THANK you very sincerely for your address. It is with more than ordinary pleasure that I have accepted your kind invitation to take part in the ceremony which is this day to mark the first step towards the establishment of an Institution, from which I join with its warmest supporters in looking for the most advantageous results.

I cannot, indeed, doubt for a moment that the expectations of those who believe that the " value " and dignity of human labour will receive a " manifold increase, when guided by the light " of scientific knowledge," will be amply realized. And it is most gratifying to me to hear the expression of your opinion that the desire for the " keener and more comprehensive study of the " principles by which the exercise of man's pro-

" ductive powers is controlled," from which you anticipate such advantage, has been stimulated by the Great Exhibition of 1851, to my connection with which you have been pleased to allude in such flattering terms.

I cannot forget that the example of such Industrial Exhibitions had been already set by this town, and with the best results; or that to the experience so acquired the Executive Committee of the greater undertaking of '51 were much indebted in carrying that work to a successful issue. As Birmingham was thus foremost in giving a practical stimulus to the works of Art and Industry, so she is now one of the first in the field to encourage a scientific study of the principles on which those works depend for success.

I trust with you, and confidently believe, that the moral as well as the material welfare of this great community will be advanced by the union, for scientific objects, of men of all classes and of all opinions, in such institutions as that of which I am to-day to have the honour of laying the first stone. And most heartily do I join with you in congratulating the country that not even such a war as that in which we are now engaged, calculated as it is to enlist our warmest sympathies and to engage our more immediate interest, can divert Englishmen from the noble work of fostering the Arts of Peace, and endeavouring to give a wider scope to the blessings of freedom and civilization.

> [Lord CALTHORPE, the President of the Institute, proposed " The Health of PRINCE ALBERT, and the other Members " of the Royal Family."
>
> HIS ROYAL HIGHNESS replied—]

I AM much obliged to you, my Lord, for your proposing my health in such kind terms, and I cannot but be much gratified by the cordial reception which you, gentlemen, have been pleased to give to this toast.

It has been a great pleasure to me to have been able to participate, in however trifling a degree, in a work which I do not look upon as a simple act of worldly wisdom on the part of this great town and locality, but as one of the first public acknowledgments of a principle which is daily forcing its way amongst us, and is destined to play a great and important part in the future development of this nation and of the world in general: I mean the introduction of science and art as the unconscious regulators of productive industry.

The courage and spirit of enterprise with

which an immense amount of capital is embarked in industrial pursuits, and the skill and indefatigable perseverance with which these are carried on in this country, cannot but excite universal admiration; but in all our operations, whether agricultural or manufacturing, it is not *we* who operate, but the laws of nature, which we have set in operation.

It is, then, of the highest importance that we should know these laws, in order to know what we are about, and the reason why certain things are, which occur daily under our hands, and what *course* we are to pursue with regard to them.

Without such knowledge we are condemned to one of three states: either we merely go on to do things just as our fathers did, and for no better reason than because they did them so; or, trusting to some personal authority, we adopt at random the recommendation of some specific, in a speculative hope that it may answer; or lastly —and this is the most favourable case—we ourselves improve upon certain processes; but this can only be the result of an experience hardly earned and dearly bought, and which, after all, can only embrace a comparatively short space of time, and a small number of experiments.

From none of these causes can we hope for

much progress; for the mind, however ingenious, has no materials to work with, and remains in presence of phenomena, the causes of which are hidden from it.

But these laws of nature, these divine laws, are capable of being discovered and understood, and of being taught and made our own. *This is the task of science;* and, whilst science discovers and teaches these laws, art teaches their application. No pursuit is therefore too insignificant not to be capable of becoming the subject both of a science and an art.

The fine arts (as far as they relate to painting, sculpture, and architecture), which are sometimes confounded with art in general, rest on the application of the laws of form and colour, and what may be called the science of the beautiful. They do not rest on any arbitrary theory on the modes of producing pleasurable emotions, but follow fixed laws—more difficult perhaps to seize than those regulating the material world, because belonging partly to the sphere of the ideal, and of our spiritual essence, yet perfectly appreciable and teachable, both abstractedly and historically, from the works of different ages and nations.

No human pursuits make any material progress until science is brought to bear upon them.

We have seen accordingly many of them slumber for centuries upon centuries ; but from the moment that science has touched them with her magic wand, they have sprung forward, and taken strides which amaze, and almost awe, the beholder.

Look at the transformation which has gone on around us since the laws of gravitation, electricity, magnetism, and the expansive power of heat have become known to us. It has altered our whole state of existence,—one might say, the whole face of the globe. We owe this to science, and to science alone ; and she has other treasures in store for us, if we will but call her to our assistance.

It is sometimes objected by the ignorant that science is uncertain and changeable, and they point with a malicious kind of pleasure to the many exploded theories which have been superseded by others, as a proof that the present knowledge may be also unsound, and, after all, not worth having. But they are not aware that, while they think to cast blame upon science, they bestow, in fact, the highest praise upon her.

For that is precisely the difference between science and prejudice : that the latter keeps stubbornly to its position, whether disproved or not, whilst the former is an unarrestable movement towards the fountain of truth, caring little for cherished authorities or sentiments, but continually progressing, feeling no false shame at her shortcomings, but, on the contrary, the highest pleasure, when freed from an error, at having advanced another step towards the attainment of Divine truth—a pleasure not even intelligible to the pride of ignorance.

We also hear, not unfrequently, science and practice, scientific knowledge and common sense, contrasted as antagonistic. A strange error! for science is eminently practical, and must be so, as she sees and knows what she is doing, whilst mere common practice is condemned to work in the dark, applying natural ingenuity to unknown powers to obtain a known result.

Far be it from me to undervalue the creative power of genius, or to treat shrewd common sense as worthless without knowledge. But nobody will tell me that the same genius would not take an incomparably higher flight, if supplied with all the means which knowledge can impart; or that common sense does not become, in fact, only truly powerful when in possession of the materials upon which judgment is to be exercised.

The study of the laws by which the Almighty governs the Universe is therefore our bounden duty. Of these laws our great academies and seats of education have, rather arbitrarily, selected only two spheres or groups (as I may call them) as essential parts of our national education: the laws which regulate quantities and proportions, which form the subject of mathematics, and the laws regulating the expression of our thoughts, through the medium of language, that is to say, grammar, which finds its purest expression in the classical languages. These laws are most important branches of knowledge, their study trains and elevates the mind, but they are not the only ones; there are others which we cannot disregard, which we cannot do without.

There are, for instance, the laws governing the human mind, and its relation to the Divine Spirit (the subject of logic and metaphysics); there are those which govern our bodily nature and its connection with the soul (the subject of physiology and psychology); those which govern human society, and the relations between man and man (the subjects of politics, jurisprudence, and political economy); and many others.

Whilst of the laws just mentioned some have been recognized as essentials of education in different institutions, and some will, by the course of time, more fully assert their right to recognition, the laws regulating matter and form are those which will constitute the chief object of *your* pursuits; and, as the principal of subdivision of labour is the one most congenial to our age, I would advise you to keep to this speciality, and to follow with undivided attention chiefly the sciences of mechanics, physics, and chemistry, and the fine arts in painting, sculpture, and architecture.

You will thus have conferred an inestimable boon upon your country, and in a short time have the satisfaction of witnessing the beneficial results upon our national powers of production. Other parts of the country will, I doubt not, emulate your example; and I live in hope that all these institutions will some day find a central point of union, and thus complete their national organization.

Thanking you once more for having allowed me to assist at the foundation of your Institution, I, with all my heart, wish it growth, vigour, and prosperity.

ADDRESS TO THE
3rd AND 4th REGIMENTS OF THE GERMAN LEGION

AT SHORNCLIFFE, ON PRESENTING TO THEM
THEIR COLOURS.

[DECEMBER 6th, 1855.]

ES freut mich herzlich Ihnen persönlich diese Fahnen überreichen zu können, da mir diess zugleich eine Gelegenheit giebt Ihnen auszudrücken, wie sehr die Königin die Bereitwilligkeit anerkannt mit welcher Sie ihrem Rufe gefolgt und unter die Waffen getreten sind.

Ich lebe der festen Ueberzeugung, dass Sie unter allen Umständen die Ehre einer Fahne aufrecht erhalten werden, die bis jetzt siegenreich in allen Theilen der Welt geweht hat, im Kampfen für Recht, Ordnung, und Freiheit, und zur Verbreitung der Civilisation.

Möge der Allmächtige Sie mit seinem Schutze in allen den Mühsalen und Gefahren begleiten, die Sie sich muthig entschlossen haben, mit der tapferen Englischen Armee zu theilen!

Sie wird Sie, daran zweifle ich nicht, als Brüder bewillkommen.

AT THE OPENING OF

THE GOLDEN-LANE SCHOOLS.

[MARCH 19TH, 1857.]

MR. ROGERS AND GENTLEMEN, PROMOTERS AND SUPPORTERS OF THESE SCHOOLS,—

I THANK you heartily for your kind and cordial welcome. I rejoice at the opportunity which has this day been afforded to me of visiting this noble establishment, and my satisfaction in doing so is increased by the circumstance that my visit occurs at a period of its existence when the state of useful development to which by your exertions it has attained is about, by a continuance of the same exertions, to receive a still wider extension. In the progress of these schools, struggling, I may say, from the most lowly and humble beginnings up to their present noble dimensions, we find a striking exemplification of the Divine truth, that the principle of good once sown is not destined to lie dormant, but that, like the grain of mustard-seed, it is calculated to extend and develop itself in an ever-increasing sphere of usefulness; and we may confidently hope that what you have now effected, following this universal law, will not be limited in its results to the immediate objects of your charitable exertions, but that it will prove the means of diffusing untold blessings among the most remote generations. For you, Mr. Rogers, who have been mainly instrumental, and at great personal sacrifice, in bringing about this great good, and for those who have stood by you, and contributed by their support to the success of your efforts, there can, I am sure, be no higher source of gratification than in the contemplation of your own work. The reflection that you have been the instrument, under Divine Providence, of conferring upon the poor and needy in this vast district that greatest of all boons, the means of obtaining for their children the blessings of education and of religious instruction, without which any lasting success in life or any permanent amelioration of their lot would seem hopeless; and still further, the feeling that this inestimable blessing will be secured in a yet higher degree to their children's children, will carry with it its own best reward. Still it will be a source of legitimate pride and satisfaction to you to know that your labours have not been unobserved, but that your noble and Christianlike exertions to benefit those who cannot help themselves have attracted the notice and admiration of your Sovereign, and of those who are deputed under her to watch over and promote the education and moral welfare of her people. The means which you have adopted to effect your work of benevolence appear no less deserving of commendation than the object itself. You have not been content with the bare attempt to force, perhaps upon unwilling recipients, a boon, the value of which might not be appreciated, but you have wisely sought to work upon the convictions of the parents of the children you wish to benefit by extending your assistance to those who, by a small contribution out of their hardly-won earnings, have proved that they are awake to a sense of the vast importance it is to their offspring that the means of being fitted to pass successfully through life, and by honest industry to better their worldly condition, should be brought within their reach. It is a source of high personal gratification to me that I have been enabled, by my presence here this day, and by that of the Prince of Wales, to mark, not only my own appreciation of your labours, but also the deep interest which the Queen takes in the well-being of the poorest of her subjects; and that gratification will be greatly enhanced if by this public expression of the sympathy of the Queen and of her family and Government this noble cause shall be still further advanced. Most earnestly do I pray that the same success which has hitherto blessed your labours may continue to attend your future progress, and that your example may stimulate other localities to emulate your useful efforts.

AT THE OPENING OF

THE EXHIBITION OF ART TREASURES
OF THE UNITED KINGDOM AT MANCHESTER.

[MAY 5TH, 1857.]

[The MAYOR of MANCHESTER having presented an Address,

His ROYAL HIGHNESS returned the following reply—]

MR. MAYOR, ALDERMEN, AND GENTLEMEN,—

I HAVE received with feelings of no ordinary gratification the address which you have presented to me, expressing such kindly feelings towards myself, and professing to represent the good wishes of the vast community which is collected in and around this city.

It will, I am sure, be most pleasing to the Queen to receive, from the expressions contained in the address, a fresh assurance of the loyal interest taken by her people in all that concerns her happiness.

I most willingly attend here this day to assist at a ceremony which the inhabitants of Manchester may well witness with pride, as its object is to inaugurate an Exhibition collected by the exertion of their enterprise and public spirit, and intended, not for the amusement and gratification of the neighbourhood alone, but for the instruction and improvement of the nation at large.

You justly allude in terms of gratitude to that comprehensive and liberal spirit which has adorned the walls of this building with the choicest specimens of art from so many private galleries of the kingdom. It added much to the pleasure with which the Queen and myself had complied with the application for works of art belonging to us when we found this example so generally followed by the possessors of treasures which are, in general, so reluctantly intrusted by their owners to the care of others.

The Queen will, I am confident, be glad again to visit Manchester, not only to mark by her presence her approval of the object and successful execution of this great undertaking which we have this day to celebrate, but from a recollection of the enthusiastic loyalty exhibited when she had formerly an opportunity of visiting this great centre of industry.

[Lord Overstone having read the Address of the General Council,

His Royal Highness replied as follows—]

My Lord and Gentlemen,—

YOU are very kind in thinking at this moment of the bereavement which has befallen the Queen and her family.

In the Duchess of Gloucester we have all lost, not only the last of the children of that good King who occupied the throne during sixty years, and carried this country fearlessly and successfully through the most momentous struggles of its history, and thus the last personal link with those times, but also a lady whose virtues and qualities of the heart had commanded the respect and love of all who knew her.

If I have thought it my duty to attend here to-day, although her mortal remains have not yet been carried to their last place of rest, my decision has been rendered easy by the conviction that, could her own opinions and wishes have been known, she would, with that sense of duty and patriotic feeling which so much distinguished her and the generation to which she belonged, have been anxious that I should not on her account, or from private feelings, disturb an arrangement intended for the public good.

[Mr. FAIRBAIRN having presented the Address of the Executive Committee,

His ROYAL HIGHNESS returned the following reply—]

GENTLEMEN OF THE EXECUTIVE COMMITTEE,—

I THANK you most sincerely for your kind address.

The expressions of loyalty and attachment to

the Queen which it conveys will, I feel certain, be most gratifying to her.

I have with pleasure accepted your invitation to preside at the inaugural ceremony of an undertaking which I have watched with the deepest interest from its first conception; and I may now be allowed to congratulate you upon the success which has so far crowned your labours.

The building in which we are assembled, and the wonderful collection of those treasures of art, as you so justly term them, which it displays, reflect the highest credit upon you. They must strike the beholder with grateful admiration, not only of the wealth and spirit of enterprise of this country, but also of that generous feeling of mutual confidence and goodwill between the different classes of society within it, of which it affords so gratifying a proof.

We behold a feast which the rich, and they who have, set before those to whom fortune has denied the higher luxuries of life—bringing forth from the innermost recesses of their private dwellings, and intrusting to your care, their choicest and most cherished treasures, in order to gratify the nation at large: and this, too, unhesitatingly, at your mere request, satisfied that your plans were disinterested and well matured, and that they had the good of the country for their object.

This is a gratifying sight, and blessed is the country in which it is witnessed. But not less so is the fact which has shown itself in this as in other instances, that the great and noble of the land look to their Sovereign to head and lead them in such patriotic undertakings; and when they see that the Sovereign has come forward to give her countenance and assistance to the work, that they feel it a pleasure to co-operate with her and not to leave her without their support— emulating thus, in works of peace, the chivalric spirit which animated their forefathers in the warlike times of old.

You have done well not to aim at a mere accumulation of works of art and objects of general interest, but to give to your collection, by a scientific and historical arrangement, an educational character,—thus not losing the opportunity of teaching the mind, as well as gratifying the senses. And manifold are the lessons which it will present to us! If art is the purest expression of the state of mental and religious culture, and of general civilization, of any age or people, an historical and chronological review given at one glance cannot fail to impress us with a just appreciation of the peculiar characteristics of the different periods and countries the works of which are here exhibited to us, and of the influence which they have exercised upon each other.

In comparing these works with those of our own age and country, while we may well be proud of the immense development of knowledge and power of production which we possess, we have reason also for humility in contemplating the refinement of feeling and intensity of thought manifested in the works of the older schools.

I trust that you may reap, in the approbation of the public at large, and in the remunerative concourse of the people, the immediate reward of your labours; and that, like the Exhibition of 1851, to which you so flatteringly allude, you may thus also find the means of closing your operations without having recourse to the Guarantee Fund which this district has so generously put at your disposal.

Beyond this, however, I trust that the beneficial effects upon the progress of art and taste in our country, which we may confidently look to, may be a lasting memorial of your vast enterprise.

AT THE OPENING OF THE

CONFERENCE ON NATIONAL EDUCATION.

[JUNE 22ND, 1857.]

GENTLEMEN,—

WE have met to-day in the sacred cause of Education—of National Education. This word, which means no less than the moral and intellectual development of the rising generation, and, therefore, the national welfare, is well calculated to engross our minds, and opens a question worthy of a nation's deepest interest and most anxious consideration. Gentlemen, the nation is alive to its importance, and our presence here to-day gives further evidence (if such evidence were needed) of its anxiety to give it that consideration. Looking to former times, we find that our forefathers, with their wonted piety and paternal care, had established a system of national education, based upon the parish organization, and forming part of parish life, which met the wants of their day, and had in it a certain unity and completeness which we may well envy at the present moment. But in the progress of time our wants have outstripped that system, and the condition of the country has so completely changed, even within these last fifty years, that the old parochial division is no longer adequate for the present population. This has increased during that period in England and Wales from, in round numbers, 9,000,000 to 18,000,000, and, where there formerly existed comparatively small towns and villages, we now see mighty cities, like Liverpool, Manchester, Hull, Leeds, Birmingham, and others, with their hundreds of thousands, springing up almost, as it were, by enchantment; London having increased to nearly two and a half million of souls, and the factory district of Lancashire alone having aggregated a population of nearly 3,000,000 within a radius of thirty miles. This change could not escape the watchful eye of a patriotic public; but how to provide the means of satisfying the new wants could not be a matter of easy solution. While zeal for the public good, a fervent religious spirit, and true philanthropy are qualities eminently distinguishing our countrymen, the love of liberty, and an aversion from being controlled by the power of the State in matters nearest to their hearts, are feelings which will always most powerfully influence them in action. Thus the common object has been contemplated from the most different points of view, and pursued often upon antagonistic principles. Some have sought the aid of Government, others that of the Church to which they belong; some have declared it to be the duty of the State to provide elementary instruction for the people at large, others have seen in the State interference a check to the spontaneous exertions of the people themselves, and an interference with self-government; some, again, have advocated a plan of compulsory education based upon local self-government, and others the voluntary system in its widest development. While these have been some of the political subjects of difference, those in the religious field have not been less marked and potent. We find, on the one hand, the wish to see secular and religious instruction separated, and the former recognized as an innate and inherent right, to which each member of society has a claim, and which ought not to be denied to him if he refuses to take along with it the inculcation of a particular dogma to which he objects as unsound; while we see, on the other hand, the doctrine asserted, that no education can be sound which does not rest on religious instruction, and that religious truth is too sacred to be modified and tampered with, even in its minutest deductions, for the sake of procuring a general agreement.

Gentlemen, if these differences were to have been discussed here to-day, I should not have been able to respond to your invitation to take the chair, as I should have thought it inconsistent with the position which I occupy, and with the duty which I owe to the Queen and the country at large. I see those here before me who have taken a leading part in these important discussions, and I am happy to meet them upon a neutral ground; happy to find that there *is* a neutral ground upon which their varied talents and abilities can be brought to bear in communion upon the common object; and proud and grateful to them that they should have allowed me to preside over them for the purpose of working together in the common vineyard. I feel certain that the greatest benefit must arise to the cause we have all so much at heart by the mere free exchange of your thoughts and various experience. You may well be proud, gentlemen, of the results hitherto achieved by your rival efforts, and may point to the fact that, since the beginning of the century, while the population has doubled itself, the number of schools, both public and private, has been multiplied fourteen times. In 1801 there were in England and Wales, of public schools, 2876; of private schools, 487—total, 3363. In 1851 (the year of the census) there were in England and Wales, of public schools, 15,518; of private schools, 30,524—total, 46,042; giving instruction in all to 2,144,378 scholars; of whom 1,422,982 belong to public schools, and 721,396 to the private schools. The rate of progress is further illustrated by statistics which show that in 1818 the proportion of day-scholars to the population was 1 in 17; in 1833, 1 in 11; and in 1851, 1 in 8. These are great results, although I hope they may only be received as instalments of what has yet to be done. But what must be your feelings when you reflect upon the fact, the inquiry into which has brought us together, that this great boon thus obtained for the mass of the people, and which is freely offered to them, should have been only partially accepted, and, upon the whole, so insufficiently applied as to render its use almost valueless! We are told that, the total population in England and Wales of children between the ages of 3 and 15 being estimated at 4,908,696, only

2,046,848 attend school at all, while 2,861,848 receive no instruction whatever. At the same time an analysis of the scholars with reference to the length of time allowed for their school tuition, shows that 42 per cent. of them have been at school for less than one year, 22 per cent. during one year, 15 per cent. during two years, 9 per cent. during three years, 5 per cent. during four years, and 4 per cent. during five years. Therefore, out of the two millions of scholars alluded to, more than one million and a half remain only two years at school. I leave it to you to judge what the results of such an education can be. I find further that of these two millions of children attending school only about 600,000 are above the age of nine.

Gentlemen, these are startling facts, which render it evident that no extension of the means of education will be of any avail unless this evil, which lies at the root of the whole question, be removed, and that it is high time that the country should become thoroughly awake to its existence, and prepared to meet it energetically. To impress this upon the public mind is the object of our conference. Public opinion is the powerful lever which in these days moves a people for good and for evil, and to public opinion we must therefore appeal if we would achieve any lasting and beneficial results. You, gentlemen, will richly add to the services which you have already rendered to the noble cause if you will prepare public opinion by your inquiry into this state of things, and by discussing in your sections the causes of it as well as the remedies which may lie within our reach. This will be no easy matter; but even if your labours should not result in the adoption of any immediate practical steps, you will have done great good in preparing for them. It will probably happen that, in this instance as in most others, the cause which produces the evil will be more easily detected than its remedy, and yet a just appreciation of the former must ever be the first and essential condition for the discovery of the latter. You will probably trace the cause of our social condition to a state of ignorance and lethargic indifference on the subject among parents generally; but the root of the evil will, I suspect, be found to extend into that field on which the political economist exercises his activity—I mean the labour market—demand and supply. To dissipate that ignorance and rouse from that lethargy may be difficult; but with the united and earnest efforts of all who are the friends of the working classes it ought, after all, to be only a question of time. What measures can be brought to bear upon the other root of the evil is a more delicate question, and will require the nicest care in handling, for there you cut into the very quick of the working man's condition. His children are not only his offspring, to be reared for a future independent position, but they constitute part of his productive power, and work with him for the staff of life; the daughters especially are the handmaids of the house, the assistants of the mother, the nurses of the younger children, the aged, and the sick. To deprive the labouring family of their help would be almost to paralyse its domestic existence. On the other hand, carefully collected statistics reveal to us the fact, that, while about 600,000 children between the ages of 3 and 15 are absent from school, but known to be employed, no less than 2,200,000 are not at schools, whose absence cannot be traced to any ascertained employment or other legitimate cause. You will have to work, then, upon the minds and hearts of the parents, to place before them the irreparable mischief which they inflict upon those who are intrusted to their care by keeping them from the light of knowledge, to bring home to their conviction that it is their duty to exert themselves for their children's education, bearing in mind at the same time that it is not only their most sacred duty, but also their highest privilege. Unless they work with you, your work, our work, will be vain; but you will not fail, I feel sure, in obtaining their co-operation if you remind them of their duty to their God and Creator. Our Heavenly Father, in His boundless goodness, has made His creatures that they should be happy, and in His wisdom has fitted His means to His ends, giving to all of them different qualities and faculties, in using and developing which they fulfil their destiny, and, running their uniform course according to His prescription, they find that happiness which He has intended for them. Man alone is born into this world with faculties far nobler than the other creatures, reflecting the image of Him who has willed that there should be beings on earth to know and worship Him, but endowed with the power of self-determination, having reason given him for his guide. He can develop his faculties, place himself in harmony with his Divine prototype, and attain that happiness which is offered to him on earth, to be completed hereafter in entire union with

Him through the mercy of Christ. But he can also leave these faculties unimproved, and miss his mission on earth. He will then sink to the level of the lower animals, forfeit happiness, and separate from his God, whom he did know how to find. Gentlemen, I say man has no right to do this—he has no right to throw off the task which is laid upon him for his happiness; it is his duty to fulfil his mission to the utmost of his power; but it is our duty, the duty of those whom Providence has removed from this awful struggle and placed beyond this fearful danger, manfully, unceasingly, and untiringly to aid by advice, assistance, and example the great bulk of the people, who, without such aid, must almost inevitably succumb to the difficulty of their task. They will not cast from them the aiding hand, and the Almighty will bless the labours of those who work in His cause.

OPENING ADDRESS

AT THE

MEETING IN THE COLLEGE OF PHYSICIANS

FOR THE

INAUGURATION OF JENNER'S STATUE.

[MAY 17TH, 1858.]

1.

GENTLEMEN,—

YOU have invited me to take the chair at this meeting, convened on the anniversary of Jenner's birth for the purpose of doing honour to his memory; and I have not hesitated to comply with your request, in order to mark, in common with you, my sense of the inestimable boon which this great philosopher and philanthropist has bestowed upon the human race.

His discovery was not the result of accident, like many others, however important, but that of long and thoughtful observation and reflection, and of continuous induction from numerous facts and carefully conducted experiments, to which a whole life had been directed. He has thus been enabled to save by his discovery more human lives than has fallen to the lot of any other man, and England has just reason to be proud to number him amongst her sons. Whilst his contemporaries testify their feeling of gratitude to him by several important public acts, it has been reserved to us to prove that we do not less highly appreciate his services, by raising a statue to his memory. May it be long preserved to exhibit the features of this benefactor of mankind to succeeding generations!

2.

I return you my best thanks for the kind words which you have spoken, and assure you that I shall feel most happy if the result of this day's meeting should be to rouse afresh public attention to the means of safety which science has placed at man's command, and the neglect of which still costs this country alone no less than annually 5000 victims.

AT THE TRINITY HOUSE.

[JULY 3RD, 1858.]

1.

"THE QUEEN."

MAY she long continue in the possession of that great blessing, "The love of her "people!"

2.

I have to propose to you the Health of " The " Prince of Wales," and the rest of the " Royal " Family."

Since I last met you here, it has pleased the Almighty to take the last of the children of King George the Third from amongst us, in the beloved and revered Duchess of Gloucester; another daughter has been vouchsafed to the Queen; and our eldest child has, united to a husband of her choice—and, I may say, worthy of her choice— passed to a distant country, where I was happy to find her the other day in the possession of every domestic blessing. The interest and sympathy evinced by the people of this country in this marriage could not but be most gratifying to the feelings of her parents.

3.

The toast which I now propose to you is the "Army and Navy."

If this toast must at all times be received by Englishmen with feelings of pride and satisfaction, who could approach it at the present moment without being also penetrated by those of admiration and deep thankfulness for the heroic deeds and sacrifices with which our gallant troops are now struggling, not only for the honour and interests of our country, but I trust for the cause of civilization and the future happiness of millions of people now unfortunately in part our enemies! May the Almighty continue to watch over our brave countrymen in the East, and grant them uninterrupted victory! His hand becomes most apparent when we consider how small are the means with which so much has been achieved. The deepest responsibility, however, attaches to us, not to rest satisfied with the enjoyment of the advantages and successes obtained by such self-sacrificing devotion, but to take care that, by maintaining these noble services in sufficient numbers, the tasks which for our benefit may be from time to time imposed upon them, should not carry with them the almost certain immolation of those who are expected to perform them.

6.

I propose to you " the Health of Her Majesty's " Ministers and the Earl of Derby."

They are called upon to administer and advise the Sovereign upon the multifarious and complicated affairs of this vast empire. In these days, moreover, when the progress of education and civilization renders the influence of public opinion upon the conduct of the Government more and more powerful, the latter has this difficult problem to solve: it has to maintain a judicious and beneficial harmony between its own conscientious convictions, and the impulsive and varying character of that public opinion.

If I might in this room be allowed to make use of a nautical metaphor, I should compare the governing body with a vessel, of which public opinion is the rudder. Should their nautical action not be most nicely adjusted, one of two results must follow—either the vessel would refuse to answer her helm, and to take the desired course; or she would answer it too quickly, which I believe you call wild steering, the effects of which may be seen in the zigzag line of the wake.

Nothing, however, can tend more to facilitate the difficult task of the Government, than that their motives and intentions should be understood and appreciated by their fellow-countrymen; and it is on occasions like the present that these can testify those feelings. With this view I now ask you to drink to the " Health of Her " Majesty's Ministers."

N.B.—Nos. 4 and 5 were answers to " My " Health," and " Prosperity to the Trinity " House." I read extracts of Reports on all business connected with the Corporation.

SPEECH DELIVERED AT CHERBOURG

AFTER THE

BANQUET ON BOARD "LA BRETAGNE."

[AUGUST 5TH, 1858.]

LA Reine désire que j'exprime à Votre Majesté combien elle est sensible à la nouvelle preuve d'amitié que vous venez de lui donner, en lui portant un toast, et en prononçant des paroles qui lui resteront chères à jamais.

Votre Majesté connait les sentiments d'amitié qu'elle vous porte, à vous, Sire, et à l'Impératrice, et je n'ai pas besoin de vous les rappeler. Vous savez également que la bonne entente entre nos deux pays est l'objet constant de ses désirs, comme il l'est des vôtres. La Reine est donc doublement heureuse d'avoir l'occasion, par sa présence ici en ce moment, de s'allier à vous, Sire, en tâchant de reserrer, autant que possible, les liens d'amitié entre les deux peuples. Cette amitié est la base de leur prospérité mutuelle, et la bénédiction du Ciel ne lui manquera pas!

La Reine porte la santé de l'Empereur et de l'Impératrice!

ON PRESENTING NEW COLOURS

TO THE

2ND BATTALION OF THE 13TH ("PRINCE ALBERT'S OWN") LIGHT INFANTRY,

AT HARFORD RIDGE, NEAR ALDERSHOT.

[FEBRUARY 21st, 1859.]

THE act which has just been performed, simple as it is, has the highest significance for the soldier! You have received in these colours the emblems of your country and your Sovereign, and of your regiment as a part of the British Army. It is your country's, your Sovereign's, and that army's honour which is bound up in them, and which you will henceforth have to guard and to defend; not by your valour alone in action, and your endurance under the hardships of campaigns, but also during the monotonous duties of peace and under the temptations of inaction—placed in different societies, under different climes, and in different parts of the world.

The British soldier has to follow these colours to every part of the globe, and everywhere he is the representative of his country's power, freedom, loyalty, and civilization. The 13th has a fair name in the world, won chiefly in distant lands— the West Indies, America, Africa, and Asia; and its defence of Jellalabad has proved that it is capable of evincing the highest qualities of the soldier. You may point with just pride to the fact that those qualities, displayed so conspicuously under Sir Robert Sale, were but now exhibited to the admiration of mankind by Sir Henry Havelock, an officer trained in its ranks!

You are a new, a young battalion, sprung with surprising rapidity together with others from a patriotic people, for the rescue of the country's mightiest interests threatened in the East. During the short time you have been together you have worked hard to assume the honourable position intrusted to you, and I may now congratulate you on your success. That the military authorities should think you fit and worthy to take your place in the Army of the Cape, shows that your exertions are appreciated and that entire confidence is reposed in you.

I feel proud that you should bear my name to that promising country.

May God's best blessing attend you, shield you from danger, support you under difficulties, cheer you under privations, grant you moderation in success, contentment under discipline, humility and gratitude towards Him in prosperity!

AT THE MEETING OF

THE BRITISH ASSOCIATION FOR THE ADVANCEMENT OF SCIENCE.

[HELD AT ABERDEEN, SEPTEMBER 14TH, 1859.]

GENTLEMEN OF THE BRITISH ASSOCIATION,—

YOUR kind invitation to me to undertake the office of your President for the ensuing year could not but startle me on its first announcement. The high position which Science occupies, the vast number of distinguished men who labour in her sacred cause, and whose achievements, while spreading innumerable benefits, justly attract the admiration of mankind, contrasted strongly in my mind with the consciousness of my own insignificance in this respect. I, a simple admirer, and would-be student of Science, to take the place of the chief and spokesman of the scientific men of the day, assembled in furtherance of their important objects!—the thing appeared to me impossible. Yet, on reflection, I came to the conclusion that, if not as a contributor to, or director of your labours, I might still be useful to you, useful to science, by accepting your offer. Remembering that this Association is a popular Association, not a secret confraternity of men jealously guarding the mysteries of their profession, but inviting the uninitiated, the public at large, to join them, having as one of its objects to break down those imaginary and hurtful barriers which exist between men of science and so-called men of practice—I felt that I could, from the peculiar position in which Providence has placed me in this country, appear as the representative of that large public, which profits by and admires your exertions, but is unable actively to join in them; that my election was an act of humility on your part, which to reject would have looked like false humility, that is like pride, on mine. But I reflected further, and saw in my acceptance the means, of which necessarily so few are offered to Her Majesty, of testifying to you, through the instrumentality of her husband, that your labours are not unappreciated by your Sovereign, and that she wishes her people to know this as well as yourselves. Guided by these reflections, my choice was speedily made, for the path of duty lay straight before me.

If these, however, are the motives which have induced me to accept your flattering offer of the Presidency, a request on my part is hardly necessary that you will receive my efforts to fulfil its duties with kind indulgence.

If it were possible for anything to make me still more aware how much I stand in need of this indulgence, it is the recollection of the person whom I have to succeed as your President—a man of whom this country is justly proud, and whose name stands among the foremost of the naturalists in Europe for his patience in investigation, conscientiousness in observation, boldness of imagination, and acuteness in reasoning. You have no doubt listened with pleasure to his parting address, and I beg to thank him for the flattering manner in which he has alluded to me in it.

The Association meets for the first time to-day in these regions and in this ancient and interesting city. The poet, in his works of fiction, has to choose, and anxiously to weigh, where to lay his scene, knowing that, like the painter, he is thus laying in the background of his picture, which will give tone and colour to the whole. The stern and dry reality of life is governed by the same laws, and we are here living, feeling, and thinking under the influence of the local impressions of this northern seaport. The choice appears to me a good one. The travelling philosophers have had to come far; but in approaching the Highlands of Scotland they meet nature in its wild and primitive form, and nature is the object of their studies. The geologist will not find many novelties in yonder mountains, because he will stand there on the bare backbone of the globe; but the primary rocks, which stand out in their nakedness, exhibit the grandeur and beauty of their peculiar form, and in the splendid quarries of this neighbourhood are seen to peculiar advantage the closeness and hardness of their mass, and their inexhaustible supply for the use of man, made available by the application of new mechanical powers. On this primitive soil the botanist and zoologist will be attracted only by a limited range of plants and animals; but they are the very species which the extension of agriculture and increase of population are gradually driving out of many parts of the country. On those blue hills the red deer, in vast herds, holds undisturbed dominion over the wide heathery forest, until the sportsman, fatigued and unstrung by the busy life of the bustling town, invades the moor, to regain health and vigour by measuring his strength with that of the antlered monarch of the hill. But, notwithstanding all his efforts to overcome an antagonist possessed of such superiority of power, swiftness, caution, and keenness of all the senses, the sportsman would find himself baffled, had not science supplied him the telescope and those terrible weapons which seem daily to progress in the precision with which they carry the deadly bullet, mocking distance, to the mark.

In return for the help which Science has afforded him, the sportsman can supply the naturalist with many facts which he alone has opportunity of observing, and which may assist the solution of some interesting problems suggested by the life of the deer. Man also, the highest object of our study, is found in vigorous, healthy development, presenting a happy mixture of the Celt, Goth, Saxon, and Dane, acquiring his strength on the hills and the sea. The Aberdeen whaler braves the icy regions of the Polar Sea, to seek and to battle with the great monster of the deep: he has materially assisted in opening these icebound regions to the researches of Science; he fearlessly aided in the search after Sir John Franklin and his gallant companions, whom their country sent forth on this mission, but to whom Providence, alas! has denied the reward of their labours, the return to their homes, to the affectionate embrace of their families and friends, and the acknowledgments of a grateful nation. The city of Aberdeen itself is rich in interest for the philosopher. Its two lately united Universities make it a seat of learning and science. The collection of antiquities, formed for the present occasion, enables him to dive into olden times, and, by contact with the remains of the handiworks of the ancient inhabitants of Scotland, to enter into the spirit of that peculiar and interesting people, which has always attracted the attention and touched the hearts of men accessible to the influence of heroic poetry. The Spalding Club, founded in this city for the preservation of the historical and literary remains of the north-eastern counties of Scotland, is honourably known by its important publications.

Gentlemen!—This is the twenty-ninth anniversary of the foundation of this Association; and well may we look back with satisfaction to its operation and achievements throughout the time of its existence. When, on the 27th of September, 1831, the meeting of the Yorkshire

Philosophical Society took place at York, in the theatre of the Yorkshire Museum, under the presidency of the late Earl Fitzwilliam, then Viscount Milton, and the Rev. W. Vernon Harcourt eloquently set forth the plan for the formation of a British Association for the Promotion of Science, which he showed to have become a want for his country, the most ardent supporter of this resolution could not have anticipated that it would start into life full-grown as it were, enter at once upon its career of usefulness, and pursue it without deviation from the original design, triumphing over the oppositions which it had to encounter in common with everything that is new and claims to be useful. Gentlemen, this proved that the want was a real, and not an imaginary one, and that the mode in which it was intended to supply that want was based upon a just appreciation of unalterable truths. Mr. Vernon Harcourt summed up the desiderata in graphic words, which have almost identically been retained as the exposition of the objects of the Society, printed at the head of the annually-appearing volume of its Transactions:—" to give a stronger " impulse and more systematic direction to " scientific inquiry—to promote the intercourse "of those who cultivate Science in different parts of the empire, with one another and with foreign philosophers—and to obtain a more general attention to the objects of Science, and a removal of any disadvantages of a public kind which impede its progress."

To define the nature of Science, to give an exact and complete definition of what that Science, to whose service the Association is devoted, is and means, has, as it naturally must, at all times occupied the Metaphysician. He has answered the question in various ways, more or less satisfactorily to himself or others. To me, Science, in its most general and comprehensive acceptation, means the knowledge of what I know, the consciousness of human knowledge. Hence, to know is the object of all Science; and all special knowledge, if brought to our consciousness in its separate distinctiveness from, and yet in its recognized relation to the totality of our knowledge, is scientific knowledge. We require, then, for Science—that is to say, for the acquisition of scientific knowledge—those two activities of our mind which are necessary for the acquisition of *any* knowledge — analysis and synthesis; the first, to dissect and reduce into its component parts the object to be investigated, and to render an accurate account to ourselves of the nature and qualities of these parts by observation; the second to recompose the observed and understood parts into a unity in our consciousness, exactly answering to the object of our investigation. The labours of the man of Science are therefore at once the most humble and the loftiest which man can undertake. He only does what every little child does from its first awakening into life, and must do every moment of its existence; and yet he aims at the gradual approximation to divine truth itself. If, then, there exists no difference between the work of the man of Science and that of the merest child, what constitutes the distinction? Merely the conscious self-determination. The child observes what accident brings before it, and unconsciously forms its notion of it; the so-called practical man observes what his special work forces upon him, and he forms his notions upon it with reference to this particular work. The man of Science observes what he intends to observe, and knows why he intends it. The value which the peculiar object has in his eyes is not determined by accident, nor by an external cause, such as the mere connection with work to be performed, but by the place which he knows this object to hold in the general universe of knowledge, by the relation which it bears to other parts of that general knowledge.

To *arrange* and *classify* that universe of knowledge becomes therefore the first, and perhaps the most important, object and duty of Science. It is only when brought into a system, by separating the incongruous and combining those elements in which we have been enabled to discover the internal connection which the Almighty has implanted in them, that we can hope to grapple with the boundlessness of His creation, and with the laws which govern both mind and matter.

The operation of Science then has been, systematically to divide human knowledge, and raise, as it were, the separate groups of subjects for scientific consideration, into different and distinct sciences. The tendency to create new sciences is peculiarly apparent in our present age, and is· perhaps inseparable from so rapid a progress as we have seen in our days; for the acquaintance with and mastering of distinct branches of knowledge enables the eye, from the newly gained points of sight, to see the new ramifications into which they divide themselves in strict consecutiveness and with logical necessity. But in thus gaining new centres of light, from which to direct our researches, and new and powerful means of adding to its ever-increasing treasures, Science approaches no nearer to the limits of its range, although travelling further and further from its original point of departure. For God's world is infinite; and the boundlessness of the universe, whose confines appear ever to retreat before our finite minds, strikes us no less with awe when, prying into the starry crowd of heaven, we find new worlds revealed to us by every increase in the power of the telescope, than when the microscope discloses to us in a drop of water, or an atom of dust, new worlds of life and animation, or the remains of such as have passed away.

Whilst the tendency to push systematic investigation in every direction enables the individual mind of man to bring all the power of which he is capable to bear on the specialities of his study, and enables a greater number of labourers to take part in the universal work, it may be feared that that consciousness of its unity which must pervade the whole of Science if it is not to lose its last and highest point of sight, may suffer. It has occasionally been given to rare intellects and the highest genius to follow the various sciences in their divergent roads, and yet to preserve that point of sight from which alone their totality can be contemplated and directed. Yet how rare is the appearance of such gifted intellects! and if they be found at intervals, they remain still single individuals, with all the imperfections of human nature.

The only mode of supplying with any certainty this want, is to be sought in the combination of men of Science representing all the specialities, and working together for the common object of preserving that unity and presiding over that general direction. This has been to some extent done in many countries by the establishment of academies embracing the whole range of the sciences, whether physical or metaphysical, historical or political. In the absence of such an institution in this country, all lovers of Science must rejoice at the existence and activity of this Association, which embraces in its sphere of action, if not the whole range of the sciences, yet a very large and important section of them, those known as the *inductive sciences*, excluding all that are not approached by the inductive method of investigation. It has, for instance (and, considering its peculiar organization and mode of action, perhaps not unwisely), eliminated from its consideration and discussions those which come under the description of moral and political sciences. This has not been done from undervaluing their importance and denying their sacred right to the special attention of mankind, but from a desire to deal with those subjects only which can be reduced to positive proof, and do not rest on opinion or faith. The subjects of the moral and political sciences involve not only opinions but feelings; and their discussion frequently rouses passions. For feelings are "subjective," as the German metaphysician has it—they are inseparable from the individual being—an attack upon them is felt as one upon the person itself; whilst facts are "objective" and belong to everybody—they remain the same facts at all times and under all circumstances: they can be proved; they have to be proved, and, when proved, are finally settled. It is with facts only that the Association deals. There may for a time exist differences of opinion on these also, but the process of removing them and resolving them into agreement is a different one from that in the moral and political sciences. These are generally approached by the *deductive* process; but if the reasoning be ever so acute and logically correct, and the point of departure, which may be arbitrarily selected, is disputed, no agreement is possible; whilst we proceed here by the *inductive* process, taking nothing on trust, nothing for granted, but reasoning upwards from the meanest fact established, and making every step sure before going one beyond it, like the engineer in his approaches to a fortress. We thus gain ultimately a roadway, a ladder by which even a child may, almost without knowing it, ascend to the summit of truth and obtain that immensely wide and extensive view which is spread below the feet of the astonished beholder. This road has been shown us by the great Bacon; and who can contemplate the prospects which it opens, without almost falling into a trance similar to that in which he allowed his imagination to wander over future ages of discovery!

From amongst the political sciences it has been attempted in modern times to detach one which admits of being severed from individual political opinions, and of being reduced to abstract laws derived from well-authenticated facts. I mean Political Economy, based on general statistics. A new Association has recently been formed, imitating our perambulating habits, and striving to comprehend in its investigations and discussions even a still more extended range of subjects, in what is called "Social Science." These efforts deserve our warmest approbation and good will. May they succeed in obtaining a purely and strictly scientific character! Our own Association has, since its meeting at Dublin, recognized the growing claims of Political Economy to scientific brotherhood, and admitted it into its Statistical Section. It could not have done so under abler guidance and happier auspices than the presidency of the Archbishop of Dublin, Dr. Whately, whose efforts in this direction are so universally appreciated. But even in this section, and whilst statistics alone were treated in it, the Association as far back as 1833 made it a rule that, in order to ensure positive results, only those classes of facts should be admitted which were capable of being expressed by numbers, and which promised, when sufficiently multiplied, to indicate general laws.

If, then, the main object of Science—and I beg to be understood, henceforth, as speaking only of that section which the Association has under its special care, viz. Inductive Science—if, I say, the object of Science is the discovery of the laws which govern natural phænomena, the primary condition for its success is: accurate observation and collection of facts in such comprehensiveness and completeness as to furnish the philosopher with the necessary material from which to draw safe conclusions.

Science is not of yesterday. We stand on the shoulders of past ages, and the amount of observations made, and facts ascertained, has been transmitted to us and carefully preserved in the various storehouses of Science; other crops have been reaped, but still lie scattered on the field; many a rich harvest is ripe for cutting, but waits for the reaper. Economy of labour is the essence of good husbandry, and no less so in the field of Science. Our Association has felt the importance of this truth, and may well claim, as one of its principal merits, the constant endeavour to secure that economy.

One of the latest undertakings of the Association has been, in conjunction with the Royal Society, to attempt the compilation of a classified catalogue of scientific memoirs, which, by combining under one head the titles of all memoirs written on a certain subject, will, when completed, enable the student who wishes to gain information on that subject to do so with the greatest ease. It gives him, as it were, the plan of the house, and the key to the different apartments in which the treasures relating to his subject are stored, saving him at once a painful and laborious search, and affording him at the same time an assurance that what is here offered contains the whole of the treasures yet acquired.

While this has been one of its latest attempts, the Association has from its very beginning kept in view that its main sphere of usefulness lay in that concentrated attention to all scientific operations which a general gives to the movements of his army, watching and regulating the progress of his impetuous soldiers in the different directions to which their ardour may have led them, carefully noting the gaps which may arise from their independent and eccentric action, and attentively observing what impediments may have stopped, or may threaten to stop, the progress of certain columns.

Thus it attempts to fix and record the position and progress of the different labours, by its Reports on the state of Sciences published annually in its Transactions;—thus it directs the attention of the labourers to those gaps which require to be filled up, if the progress is to be a safe and steady one;—thus it comes forward with a helping hand in striving to remove those impediments which the unaided efforts of the individual labourer have been or may be unable to overcome.

Let us follow the activity of the Association in these three different directions.

The Reports on the state of Science originate in the conviction of the necessity for fixing, at given intervals, with accuracy and completeness, the position at which it has arrived. For this object the General Committee of the Association intrusts to distinguished individuals in the different branches of Science the charge of becoming, as it were, the biographers of the period. There are special points in different Sciences in which it sometimes appears desirable to the different Sections to have special Reports elaborated; in such cases the General Committee, in its capacity of the representative assembly of all the Sciences, reserves to itself the right of judging what may be of sufficient importance to be thus recorded.

The special subjects which the Association points out for investigation, in order to supply the gaps which it may have observed, are— either such as the philosopher alone can successfully investigate, because they require the close attention of a practised observer, and a thorough knowledge of the particular subject; or they are such as require the greatest possible number of facts to be obtained. Here Science often stands in need of the assistance of the general public, and gratefully accepts any contributions offered, provided the facts be accurately observed. In either case the Association points out *what* is to be observed, and *how* it is to be observed.

The first is the result of the same careful sifting process which the Association employs in directing the issue of special Reports. The investigations are intrusted to specially-appointed committees, or selected individuals. They are in most cases not unattended with considerable expense, and the Association, not content with merely suggesting and directing, furnishes by special grants the pecuniary means for defraying the outlay caused by the nature and extent of the inquiry. If we consider that the income of the Association is solely derived from the contributions of its members, the fact that no less a sum than 17,000*l*. has, since its commencement, been thus granted for scientific purposes, is certainly most gratifying.

The question *how* to observe, resolves itself into two—that of the scientific method which is to be employed in approaching a problem or in making an observation, and that of the philosophical instruments used in the observation or experiment. The Association brings to bear the combined knowledge and experience of the scientific men, not only of this but of other countries, on the discovery of that method which, while it economizes time and labour, promises the most accurate results. The method to which, after careful examination, the palm has been awarded, is then placed at the free disposal and use of all scientific investigators. The Association also issues, where practicable, printed forms, merely requiring the different heads to be filled up, which, by their uniformity, become an important means for assisting the subsequent reduction of the observations for the abstraction of the laws which they may indicate.

At the same time most searching tests and inquiries are constantly carried on in the Observatory at Kew, given to the Association by Her Majesty, the object of which is practically to test the relative value of different methods and instruments, and to guide the constantly progressive improvements in the construction of the latter.

The establishment at Kew has undertaken the

further important service of verifying and correcting to a fixed standard the instruments of any maker, to enable observations made with them to be reduced to the same numerical expression. I need hardly remind the inhabitants of Aberdeen that the Association, in one of the first years of its existence, undertook the comparative measurement of the Aberdeen standard scale with that of Greenwich,—a research ably carried out by the late Mr. Baily.

The impediments to the general progress of Science, the removal of which I have indicated as one of the tasks which the Association has set for itself, are of various kinds. If they were only such as direction, advice, and encouragement would enable the individual, or even combined efforts of philosophers, to overcome, the exertions of the Association which I have just alluded to might be sufficient for the purpose. But they are often such as can only be successfully dealt with by the powerful arm of the State or the long purse of the nation. These impediments may be caused either by the social condition of the country itself, by restrictions arising out of peculiar laws, by the political separation of different countries, or by the magnitude of the undertakings being out of all proportion to the means and power of single individuals, of the Association, or even the voluntary efforts of the public. In these cases, the Association, together with its sister society, " The Royal Society," becomes the spokesman of Science with the Crown, the Government, or Parliament—sometimes even, through the Home Government, with foreign Governments. Thus it obtained the establishment, by the British Government, of magnetic and meteorological observatories in six different parts of the globe, as the beginning of a network of stations which we must hope will be so far extended as to compass by their geographical distribution the whole of the phenomena which throw light on this important point in our tellurian and even cosmical existence. The Institute of France, at the recommendation of M. Arago, whose loss the scientific world must long deplore, cheerfully co-operated with our Council on this occasion. It was our Association which, in conjunction with the Royal Society, suggested the Antarctic Expedition, with a view to further the discovery of the laws of terrestrial magnetism, and thus led to the discovery of the southern polar continent. It urged on the Admiralty the prosecution of the tidal observations, which that department has since fully carried out. It recommended the establishment, in the British Museum, of the conchological collection exhibiting present and extinct species, which has now become an object of the greatest interest.

I will not weary you by further examples, with which most of you are better acquainted than I am myself, but merely express my satisfaction that there should exist bodies of men who will bring the well-considered and understood wants of Science before the public and the Government, who will even hand round the begging-box and expose themselves to refusals and rebuffs to which all beggars are liable, with the certainty, besides, of being considered great bores. Please to recollect that this species of bore is a most useful animal, well adapted for the ends for which Nature intended him. He alone, by constantly returning to the charge, and repeating the same truths and the same requests, succeeds in awakening attention to the cause which he advocates, and obtains that hearing which is granted him at last for self-protection, as the minor evil compared to his importunity, but which is requisite to make his cause understood. This is more particularly the case in a free, active, enterprizing, and self-determining people like ours, where every interest works for itself, considers itself the all-important one, and makes its way in the world by its own efforts. Is it, then, to be wondered at, that the interests of Science—abstract as Science appears, and not immediately showing a return in pounds, shillings, and pence—should be postponed, at least, to others which promise immediate tangible results? Is it to be wondered at, that even our public men require an effort to wean themselves from other subjects in order to give their attention to Science and men of Science, when it is remembered that Science, with the exception of mathematics, was until of late almost systematically excluded from our school and university education—that the traditions of early life are those which make and leave the strongest impression on the human mind, and that the subjects with which we become acquainted, and to which our energies are devoted in youth, are those for which we retain the liveliest interest in after years—and that for these reasons the effort required must be both a mental and a moral one? A deep debt of gratitude is therefore due to bodies like this Association, which not only urges the wants of Science on the Government, but furnishes it at once with well-matured plans how to supply them with the greatest certainty and to the greatest public advantage.

We may be justified in hoping, however, that by the gradual diffusion of Science, and its inreasing recognition as a principal part of our national education, the public in general, no less than the Legislature and the State, will more and more recognize the claims of Science to their attention; so that it may no longer require the begging-box, but speak to the State like a favoured child to its parent, sure of his parental solicitude for its welfare; that the State will recognize in Science one of its elements of strength and prosperity, to foster which the clearest dictates of self-interest demand.

If the activity of this Association, such as I have endeavoured to describe it, ever found or could find its personification in one individual—its incarnation as it were—this had been found in that distinguished and revered philosopher who has been removed from amongst us in his ninetieth year, within these last few months. Alexander von Humboldt incessantly strove after dominion over that universality of human knowledge which stands in need of thoughtful government and direction to preserve its integrity; he strove to tie up the *fasces* of scientific knowledge, to give them strength in unity. He treated all scientific men as members of one family, enthusiastically directing, fostering, and encouraging inquiry, where he saw either the want of, or the willingness for it. His protection of the young and ardent student led many to success in their pursuit. His personal influence with the Courts and Governments of most countries in Europe enabled him to plead the cause of Science in a manner which made it more difficult for them to refuse than to grant what he requested. All lovers of Science deeply mourn for the loss of such a man. Gentlemen, it is a singular coincidence, that this very day on which we are here assembled, and are thus giving expression to our admiration of him, should be the anniversary of his birth.

To return to ourselves, however: one part of the functions of the Association can receive no personal representation, no incarnation: I mean the very fact of meetings like that which we are at present inaugurating. This is not the thoughtful direction of one mind over acquired knowledge, but the production of new thought by the contact of many minds, as the spark is produced by the friction of flint and steel; it is not the action of the monarchy of a paternal Government, but the republican activity of the Roman Forum. These meetings draw forth the philosopher from the hidden recesses of his study, call in the wanderer over the field of science to meet his brethren, to lay before them the results of his labours, to set forth the deductions at which he has arrived, to ask for their examination, to maintain in the combat of debate the truth of his positions and the accuracy of his observations. These meetings, unlike those of any other Society, throw open the arena to the cultivators of all sciences, to their mutual advantage: the geologist learns from the chemist that there are problems for which he had no clue, but which that science can solve for him; the geographer receives light from the naturalist, the astronomer from the physicist and engineer, and so on. And all find a field upon which to meet the public at large,—invite them to listen to their reports and even to take part in their discussions,—show to them that philosophers are not vain theorists, but essentially men of practice —not conceited pedants, wrapped up in their own mysterious importance, but humble inquirers after truth, proud only of what they may have achieved or won for the general use of man.

Neither are they daring and presumptuous unbelievers—a character which ignorance has sometimes affixed to them—who would, like the Titans, storm heaven by placing mountain upon mountain, till hurled down from the height attained, by the terrible thunders of outraged Jove; but rather the pious pilgrims to the Holy Land, who toil on in search of the sacred shrine, in search of truth—God's truth—God's laws as manifested in His works, in His creation.

AT THE DINNER

ON THE

OPENING OF THE CLOTHWORKERS' HALL,

IN THE CITY.

[MARCH 27TH, 1860.]

Sir, and Gentlemen,—

I BEG to return you my best thanks for your kindness in drinking my health with such gratifying demonstrations of good will towards me.

It is in accordance with our nature, that, after having accomplished a task and succeeded in any work of our hands, we should banish from our minds the recollection of the troubles and anxieties which accompanied its conception and progress, and rejoice not only ourselves in our success, but ask our neighbours and friends to come and rejoice with us. We want them to see what we have done, and to share in our satisfaction.

I am grateful to you that you should have thought of including me in the number of your friends, for I can, I assure you, fully appreciate your undertaking, and honestly congratulate you on your success.

It must have cost you some hesitation and regret to separate yourselves from a hall in which your forefathers had feasted the first Kings of the House of Stuart, and in which they, as well as yourselves, habitually met for business and re-creation. But the marks of man, like the organic bodies in nature, to be preserved require to be continually renewed, and thus alone resist the destructive tendency of time; and you determined (as we see to-day) to follow Nature also in the law of increase, and to show that you have grown and expanded within these two hundred years. Your desire to see me amongst you upon this occasion, which I must attribute to your loyalty to the Queen, and my pleasure in responding to your call, proves, at the same time, that those feelings of mutual regard and affection which subsisted two hundred years ago between these great and wealthy companies, these little independent republics of the City of London, and the Crown, have withstood the effects of time, are living, ay—and I trust are even grown in intensity and warmth. In such feelings we gladly recognize one of the essential conditions of the political and social life of a free and prosperous nation.

May these blessings be preserved to this favoured land from generation to generation! and may this Corporation, of which I feel proud to have by your kindness been admitted to-day as a member, live and prosper on, as one of the important links which connect succeeding generations with those which have long passed away!

Let me drink to the health of our Master and Wardens, and Prosperity to the " Clothworkers' " Company!"

AT THE

BANQUETING-ROOM, ST. JAMES'S PALACE,

ON THE OCCASION OF THE

200TH ANNIVERSARY OF THE FORMATION
OF THE GRENADIER GUARDS.

[JUNE 16TH, 1860.]

GENTLEMEN,—

1.
"THE QUEEN."

2.

I AM much obliged to Colonel Lewis for the kind terms in which he has proposed to you to drink my health, and much gratified at the feelings which you have evinced by the manner in which you have responded to his proposal.

Gentlemen!—I was justly proud of the distinguished honour conferred upon me when I was appointed, eight years ago, to succeed the immortal Duke of Wellington in the command of this regiment, and of having since held this honourable post, which connects me with you, not only officially, but on terms of intimate and I hope cordial personal relations; but it is on an occasion like the present that the consideration must rise to my mind in its full force,—what honour and distinction is involved in the title of Colonel of the Grenadier Guards.

We are assembled to celebrate the 200th Anniversary of the formation of the Regiment as at present constituted — 200 years, which embrace the most glorious period of the history of our country—and in the most glorious events of this history the Regiment has borne an important and distinguished part. It has fought at sea and on land, in most parts of Europe, in Africa and America; and, whether fighting the French, Dutch, Spaniards, Moors, Turks, or Russians, it has stood to its colours, upheld the honour of the British name, and powerfully contributed to those successes which have, under God's blessing, made that name stand proudly forth amongst the nations of the earth.

I need not recall to your recollection its deeds, which must be all present to your minds, but I cannot forego on such an occasion pointing at least to some of the most important of the long and uninterrupted list of victories with which the Grenadier Guards have been associated. I must point to the celebrated siege and capture of Namur, the first defence of Gibraltar, the capture of Barcelona and Valencia, the battles of Blenheim, Ramillies, Oudenarde, and Malplaquet, the battle of Dettingen, ay! and of Fontenoy, where, though the victory did not ultimately remain with the Allies, it was fairly won, as far as the English were concerned, and that by the conspicuous prowess of the Grenadier Guards! the capture of Cherbourg, which, just a century ago, looked grimly across at our shores; the battles in Germany under the Marquis of Granby; the battle of Lincelles; those of Corunna, Barrosa, and the Pyrenees; the capture of St. Sebastian; battles of Nive and Nivelle, and of Waterloo, in which last great struggle with Napoleon the Regiment acquired the title of Grenadier Guards, from having defeated, in fair fight, those noble and devoted grenadiers of his Imperial Guard, who, till met by the British bayonet, had been considered invincible; and more lately the battles of the Alma and of Inkerman, and the long-protracted siege of Sevastopol.

These are glorious annals, and proud the corps may well be which can show the like! But the duty of the soldier unfortunately is not confined to fighting the foreign enemies of his country, it has at times been his fate to have to stand in arms against even his own brothers! a mournful duty, which we may trust never to see again imposed upon a British soldier. Under such circumstances he is upheld, however, by the consideration that, while he is implicitly obeying the commands of his sovereign, to whom he has sworn fidelity, he purchases, by his blood, for his country, that internal peace and that supremacy of the law upon which alone are based the liberty as well as the permanent happiness and prosperity of a nation.

The regiment, originally sprung from those loyalists who had clung to Charles the Second in exile, has never failed in its duty to its Sovereign: it fought for James the Second against Monmouth on the field of Sedgemoor; and struggled during five years heroically, although finally in vain, to preserve to George the Third his revolted American colonies.

Gentlemen! That same discipline which has made this regiment ever ready and terrible in war, has enabled it to pass long periods of peace in the midst of all the temptations of a luxurious metropolis without loss in vigour and energy,—to live in harmony and good fellowship with its brother citizens,—and to point to the remarkable fact, that the Household troops have now for 200 years formed the permanent garrison of London, have always been at the command of the civil power to support law and order, but have never themselves disturbed that order, or given cause of complaint either by insolence or licentiousness.

Let us hope that for centuries to come these noble qualities may still shine forth, and that the Almighty will continue to shield and favour this little band of devoted soldiers; let us on our part manfully do our duty, mindful of the deeds of our predecessors, loyal to our Sovereign, and jealous of the honour of our country.

I propose to you to drink " Prosperity to the " Grenadier Guards, and to the health of Colonel " Lewis, for so many years an honoured member " of the corps, and now its zealous and able " commander, and to the officers and men of the " regiment."

3.

I have to propose to you " The Health of the

" Prince of Wales, and the other members of the
" Royal Family."

The Prince was admitted into the army a year and a half ago, on his seventeenth birthday; and although his studies have as yet prevented his taking upon himself any military duty, he has while staying in Edinburgh tried to make himself acquainted with the evolutions of the cavalry by joining regularly in the drill of the 16th Lancers, quartered there at the time of his residence.

4.

The toast I wish now to propose is that of our sister-service—" The Navy."

The wooden walls of Old England have at all times been the chief defence of our country, the protection of our commerce, and constitute the link which holds together our vast and widely scattered empire. Modern science has effected greater changes in this service than perhaps in any other human pursuit, and foreign nations have, as it were, started afresh with us from the same point of departure in the race of naval preparation; but there is in Englishmen that confidence in their superiority on the unstable element, which has powerful influence in creating and maintaining it, and gives assurance of success. I believe at the same time the service never to have been in a higher state of efficiency.

5.

Let us drink to " The Army."

That army, of which the brigade of Guards, and this Regiment in it, form only a small but integral part,—integral not only from its organization, but from its spirit and feeling. The country has no less reason to be proud of its Army than of its Navy; and if in point of numbers it cannot boast of a supremacy, nay, even a comparison with other countries, it yields to none in those qualities of courage, discipline, and endurance which constitute the essential virtues of the soldier. The duties which this army has to perform in peace as well as in war could not, I make bold to say, be rendered by any other army in the world; and although it is a common doctrine that the British nation is not a military nation, I totally disbelieve that any other could furnish such an army, composed entirely of volunteers as it is.

I beg to couple this toast with the health of my dear relative, our gallant Commander-in-

Chief, who is indefatigable in his solicitude to maintain, and where possible to increase, its efficiency; and of the Queen's Secretary of State, who so ably presides over the civil administration of the Army, and has not only the sinews of war to prepare, but also that material by which science strives to reduce the individual power of man as an element in the attainment of victory, and on the superiority of which so much in war must in future depend.

"The Army, the Duke of Cambridge, and " Mr. Sidney Herbert."

6.

We are honoured by the presence of the Commanders of the other Regiments, both of cavalry and infantry, composing the Household Troops, whose services will live with yours in history, and render them worthy to be the body-guard of the Sovereign of these realms. We most painfully feel, however, the absence of one of these Commanders, whose name had been associated with the glories of the Guards in many a well-fought field. He has been called away from this temporary scene to an eternal and better world; but the memory of Sir John Byng (the Earl of Strafford) will ever be cherished by his brother officers.

The Scots Fusiliers, my personal connection with whom during ten years will always remain a proud and most pleasing recollection to me, will in a few days celebrate their jubilee as we are now doing; while the Coldstreams, true to their motto, have gained a march upon us in having had their jubilee some years before us, counting their creation from the time of the Commonwealth, when they formed General Monk's Regiment.

I beg to propose to you to drink the health of the Household Troops, and to connect with the toast the name of that gallant and distinguished general, Field Marshal Viscount Combermere.

TOAST GIVEN AT

THE DINNER OF THE TRINITY HOUSE.

[JUNE 23RD, 1860.]

1.

"THE QUEEN."

2.

I PROPOSE to drink to His Royal Highness the Prince of Wales and the rest of the Royal Family. The younger members of the Royal Family are rapidly growing up. The Princess Royal has already become the founder of a new family, destined to mount the throne of Prussia. The Prince of Wales is following his academic course at Oxford, which he intends to complete at the sister University, Cambridge; while his younger brother has, by the prescribed apprenticeship, earned his rating as Midshipman, and serves zealously as such in the Fleet. It will be a curious coincidence, that nearly at the same time—a few weeks hence—though almost at the opposite poles, the Prince of Wales will inaugurate, in the Queen's name, that stupendous work, the great bridge over the St. Lawrence in Canada, while Prince Alfred will lay the foundation stone of the breakwater for the harbour of Cape Town. What vast considerations, as regards our country, are brought to our minds in this simple fact! What present greatness! what past history! what future hopes! and how important and beneficent is the part given to the Royal Family of England to act in the development of those distant and rising countries, who recognize in the British Crown, and their allegiance to it, their supreme bond of union with the mother country and with each other!

3.

Gentlemen,—The standing toast, after that of the Royal Family, at all our public dinners, is "The Army and Navy;" and it is never given without calling forth proud and grateful feelings, for Englishmen have reason to be proud of the condition of these services, and of the deeds which they have achieved, and cause to be grateful for the benefits which have been secured to them by their soldiers and sailors, who have been drawn from all ranks and classes of society, and have devoted their lives to their country. We hear sometimes complaints of the expense which these services entail, and must certainly regret that such sacrifices should be necessary; but on the whole the public spirit with which the nation is determined, through good and evil report, to maintain the efficiency of these establishments, is a most gratifying proof of its soundness at heart and the shrewdness of its instinct. It has lately come forward, and placed at the service of the Queen, Volunteer Corps to act as an auxiliary to the regular Army and Militia, in case of danger to our shores; and the rapidity with which this movement has developed itself has been the subject of universal and just admiration. We have witnessed this day a scene which will never fade from the memory of those who had the good fortune to be present—the representatives of the independence, education, and industry of this country in arms, to testify their devotion to their country, and their readiness to lay down their lives in its defence. The Volunteer force exceeds already 130,000 men; and to what extent this country is capable of exerting itself in real danger is shown by the number of Volunteers, which in 1804 reached the extraordinary figure of 479,000! We are apt to forget, however, that, in contrast with every other country of the world, all our services are composed exclusively of volunteers: the Navy, Coast-Guard, Coast Volunteers, Army, Militia, Yeomanry, Constabulary. May the noble and patriotic spirit which such a fact reveals remain ever unimpaired! And may God's blessing, of which this nation has seen such unmistakable evidence, continue to rest upon these voluntary services! I beg to couple the toast with the names of the First Lord of the Admiralty the Duke of Somerset, and Sir John Burgoyne.

4.

I am much obliged to you for your kindness in drinking my health. I feel proud to have, by the vote of this distinguished Corporation, been re-elected its Master—an office of annual tenure, which does not tax very hard the energies of the holder, as the real work is admirably done by the Deputy Master and the Elder Brethren; but which is of the highest interest to whoever reflects upon the important and useful duties which are performed by the Corporation, the proper performance of which has so great an influence on the commercial prosperity not only of this metropolis, but of the country at large.

I cannot meet you to-day without having one recalled to my memory who used to sit on my left hand on all former occasions, and who was honoured and beloved by this Corporation, and justly so, as its Deputy Master. Captain Shepheard was one of those unobtrusive but noble characters whose sterling qualities of head and heart secured to him the confidence of all who knew him; and I can appeal to no greater proof of the estimation in which he was held than the fact that he was at once Deputy Master of this Corporation, Chairman of the East India Company, and Chairman of the Hudson's Bay Company. His successor, like himself, is an Aberdeenshire man, but, unlike him, has passed his life in the Royal Navy, and not the merchant service. I can wish him no better success than to possess the approbation of his brethren in an equal degree with his predecessor! I propose to you to drink his health, and Prosperity to the Corporation of the Trinity House.

5.

We are honoured by the presence of Her Majesty's Ministers. The Corporation is much gratified at their having found it possible, amidst the many avocations and duties which so peculiarly press upon them during the Parliamentary season, to devote an evening to the Trinity House. I propose to you to drink their health. We can wish them nothing better than good health, to enable them to withstand the fatigues of their laborious and harassing life; and by making the fullest use of their talents and energies, to gain that public recognition and confidence upon which so much of their success and usefulness must depend. This is not a political meeting, and we cautiously abstain from alluding to politics; whilst, therefore, the Ministers escape our criticism, they must also forego our praise; but we can give them what may be more valuable to them than either—the expression of our esteem and good will.

"Lord Palmerston and Her Majesty's Minis-
" ters."

6.

We must not omit to acknowledge the presence of some of our Honorary Brethren, whose admission to our body sheds lustre upon the Corporation. The known presence of their names upon our Roll gives the public an assurance that we are well thought of and well looked after by some of the best in the land.

I beg to drink to the health of Lord Derby and the Honorary Brethren.

7.

Brethren of the Trinity House,—Let us, before separating, thank our guests for the honour they have done and the pleasure they have given us by their presence at our annual dinner; and let us drink to their health and happiness. I beg to couple this toast with the name of the Duke of Newcastle.

ON OPENING THE

INTERNATIONAL STATISTICAL CONGRESS.

[HELD IN LONDON, JULY 16TH, 1860.]

GENTLEMEN,—

THE Statistical Congress of All Nations has been invited by the Government to hold its fourth meeting in this metropolis, in conformity with the wishes expressed by the late Congress held at Vienna in 1857. Although under these circumstances it would have been more properly within the province of a member of the Government, and Minister of the Crown, to fill this Chair, and open the proceedings of the day, as has been the case in previous meetings of the Congress in other places, the nature of the institutions and the habits of the people of the country in which this Assembly was to take place could not fail to make itself felt and to influence its organization. We are a people possessing and enjoying the most intense political life, in which every question of interest or importance to the nation is publicly canvassed and debated; the whole nation, as it were, from the highest to the lowest, takes an active part in these debates, and arrives at a judgment with regard to them, on the collective result of the thoughts and opinions thus called forth.

This Congress could therefore only be either a private meeting of the delegates of different Governments, discussing special questions of interest in the midst of the general bustle of political activity, or it had to assume a public and a national character, addressing itself to the public at large, and inviting its co-operation. The Government have chosen the latter alternative, and have been met by the readiest response from all sides. They have, I think, wisely chosen; for it is of the utmost importance to the object the Congress has in view—namely, not only the diffusion of statistical information, but also the acquisition of a general acknowledgment of the usefulness and importance of this branch of human knowledge—that the public, as a whole, should take up the questions which are intended to be investigated, and should lend its powerful aid.

Gentlemen, this explains, and must serve as an apology for, my presuming to hold the post of your President, for which I otherwise feel full well my unworthiness. When, however, the Commissioners for the organization of the Congress expressed to me their desire that I should do so, I felt it incumbent upon me not to withhold my individual co-operation, carrying with it, as it would, an assurance to the British people that the object of the Meeting was one which had enlisted the sympathy of their Queen, and testifying to the foreign delegates the esteem in which she holds them personally, and her appreciation of the science which they serve.

Let me now welcome them to this country, and welcome them on behalf of this country. It is here that the idea of an International Statistical Congress took its origin, when delegates and visitors from all nations had assembled to exhibit in noble rivalry the products of their science, skill, and industry, in the Great Exhibition of 1851; it is here that Statistical Science was earliest developed; and Dr. Farr has well reminded us that England has been called, by no less an authority than Bernouilli, " the cradle of poli- " tical arithmetic," and that we may even appeal to our Domesday Book as one of the most ancient and complete monuments of the science in existence. It is this country also which will and must derive the greatest benefits from the achievements of this science, and which will consequently have most cause to be grateful to you for the result of your labours.

Gentlemen, old as your science is, and undeniable as are the benefits which it has rendered to mankind, it is yet little understood by the multitude, new in its acknowledged position amongst the other sciences, and still subject to many vulgar prejudices.

It is little understood; for it is dry and unpalatable to the general public in its simple arithmetical expressions, representing living facts (which, as such, are capable of arousing the liveliest sympathy) in dry figures and tables for comparison. Much labour is required to wade through endless columns of figures, much patience to master them, and some skill to draw any definite and safe conclusions from the mass of material which it presents to the student; while the value of the information offered depends exactly upon its bulk, increasing in proportion with its quantity and comprehensiveness.

It has been little understood, also, from the peculiar and often unjustifiable use which has been made of it. For the very fact of its difficulty, and the patience required in reading up and verifying the statistical figures which may be referred to by an author in support of his theories and opinions, protect him, to a certain extent, from scrutiny, and tempt him to draw largely upon so convenient and available a capital. The public generally, therefore, connect in their minds statistics, if not with unwelcome taxation (for which they naturally form an important basis), certainly with political controversies, in which they are in the habit of seeing public men making use of the most opposite statistical results with equal assurance in support of the most opposite arguments. A great and distinguished French Minister and statesman is even quoted as having boasted of the invention of what he is said to have called "l'Art de "grouper les Chiffres." But if the same ingenuity and enthusiasm which may have suggested to him this art should have tempted him or others, as historians, to group facts also, it would be no more reasonable to make the historical facts answerable for the use made of them than it would be to make statistical science responsible for many an ingenious financial statement.

Yet this science has suffered materially in

public estimation by such use, although the very fact that statesmen, financiers, physicians, and naturalists should seek to support their statements and doctrines by statistics shows conclusively that they all acknowledge them as the foundation of truth; and this ought, therefore, to raise, instead of depressing, the science in the general esteem of the public.

Statistical Science is, as I have said, comparatively new in its position amongst the sciences in general; and we must look for the cause of this tardy recognition to the fact that it has the appearance of an incomplete science, and of being rather a helpmate to other sciences than having a right to claim that title for itself. But this is an appearance only. For if pure statistics abstain from participating in the last and highest aim of all science (viz. the discovering and expounding the laws which govern the universe), and leave this duty to their more favoured sisters the natural and the political sciences, this is done with conscious self-abnegation, for the purpose of protecting the purity and simplicity of their sacred task—the accumulation and verification of facts, unbiassed by any consideration of the ulterior use which may, or can, be made of them.

Those general laws, therefore, in the knowledge of which we recognize one of the highest treasures of man on earth, are left unexpressed, though rendered self-apparent, as they may be read in the uncompromising, rigid figures placed before him.

It is difficult to see how, under such circumstances, and notwithstanding this self-imposed abnegation, Statistical Science, as such, should be subject to prejudice, reproach, and attack; and yet the fact cannot be denied.

We hear it said that its prosecution leads necessarily to Pantheism, and the destruction of true religion, as depriving, in man's estimation, the Almighty of His power of free self-determination, making His world a mere machine working according to a general prearranged scheme, the parts of which are capable of mathematical measurement, and the scheme itself of numerical expression!—that it leads to fatalism, and therefore deprives man of his dignity, of his virtue and morality, as it would prove him to be a mere wheel in this machine, incapable of exercising a free choice of action, but predestined to fulfil a given task and to run a prescribed course, whether for good or for evil.

These are grave accusations, and would be

terrible indeed if they were true. But are they true? Is the power of God destroyed or diminished by the discovery of the fact that the earth requires three hundred and sixty-five revolutions upon its own axis to every revolution round the sun, giving us so many days to our year, and that the moon changes thirteen times during that period; that the tide changes every six hours; that water boils at a temperature of 212° according to Fahrenheit; that the nightingale sings only in April and May; that all birds lay eggs; that a hundred and six boys are born to every hundred girls? Or is man a less free agent because it has been ascertained that a generation lasts about thirty years; that there are annually posted at the Post-offices the same number of letters on which the writer had forgotten to place any address; that the number of crimes committed under the same local, national, and social conditions is constant; that the full-grown man ceases to find amusement in the sports of the child?

But our Statistical Science does not even say that this must be so; it only states that it has been so, and leaves it to the naturalist or political economist to argue that it is probable, from the number of times in which it has been found to be so, that it will be so again, as long as the same causes are operating. It thus gave birth to that part of Mathematical Science called the calculation of probabilities, and even established the theory that in the natural world there exist no certainties at all, but only probabilities. Although this doctrine, destroying man's feeling of security to a certain extent, has startled and troubled some, it is no less true that, whilst we may reckon with a thoughtless security on the sun rising to-morrow, this is only a probable event, the probability of which is capable of being expressed by a determined mathematical fraction. Our insurance offices have, from their vast collection of statistical facts, established, to such a precision, the probable duration of man's life, that they are able to enter with each individual into a precise bargain on the value of this life; and yet this does not imply an impious pretension to determine when the individual is really to die.

But we are met also by the most opposite objection; and statistics are declared *useless*, because they cannot be relied on for the determination of any given cause, and do only establish probabilities where man requires and asks for certainty. This objection is well founded; but it does not affect the science itself, but solely the use which man has in vain tried to make of it, and for which it is not intended. It is the essence of the Statistical Science, that it only makes apparent general laws, but that these laws are inapplicable to any special case; that therefore what is proved to be law in general is uncertain in particular. Herein lies the real refutation also of the first objection; and thus is the power, wisdom, and goodness of the Creator manifested, showing how the Almighty has established the physical and moral world on unchangeable laws, conformable to His eternal nature, while He has allowed to the individual the freest and fullest use of his faculties, vindicating at the same time the majesty of His laws by their remaining unaffected by individual self-determination.

Gentlemen, I am almost ashamed to speak such homely truths (of which I feel myself at best to be a very inadequate exponent) to a meeting like this, including men of such eminence in the science, and particularly in the presence of one who was your first President, M. Quetelet, and from whom I had the privilege, now twenty-four years ago, to receive my first instruction in the higher branches of mathematics—one who has so successfully directed his great abilities to the application of the science to those social phenomena, the discovery of the governing laws of which can only be approached by the accumulation and reduction of statistical facts.

It is the social condition of mankind, as exhibited by those facts, which forms the chief object of the study and investigation undertaken by this Congress; and it hopes that the results of its labours will afford to the statesman and legislator a sure guide in his endeavours to promote social development and happiness. The importance of these international Congresses in this respect cannot be overrated. They not only awaken public attention to the value of these pursuits, bring together men of all countries who devote their lives to them, and who are thus enabled to exchange their thoughts and varied experiences; but they pave the way to an agreement amongst different governments and nations to follow up these common inquiries, in a common spirit, by a common method, and for a common end.

It is only in the largest number of observations that the law becomes apparent; and the truth becomes more and more to be relied upon, the larger the amount of facts accurately observed which form the basis of its elucidation. It is consequently of the highest importance that observations identical in character should embrace the largest field of observation attainable. It is not sufficient, however, to collect the statistical facts of one class, over the greatest area, and to the fullest amount, but we require, in order to arrive at sound conclusions as to the influences operating in producing these facts, the simultaneous collection of the greatest variety of facts,—the statistics of the increase of population, of marriages, births and deaths, of emigration, disease, crime, education and occupation, of the products of agriculture, mining, and manufacture, of the results of trade, commerce, and finance. Nor, while their comparison becomes an essential element in the investigation of our social condition, does it suffice to obtain these observations as a whole, but we require also, and particularly, the comparison of these same classes of facts in different countries, under the varying influences of political and religious conditions, of occupation, races, and climates. And even this comparison of the same facts in different localities does not give us all the necessary material from which to draw our conclusions; for we require, as much as anything else, the collection of observations of the same classes of facts, in the same localities, and under the same conditions, but at different times. It is only the element of time, in the last instance, which enables us to test progress or regress—that is to say, life.

Thus the physician, by feeling the pulse of the greatest number of individuals coming under his observation, old and young, male and female, and at all seasons, arrives at the average number of the pulsations of the heart in man's normal condition : by feeling the pulse of the same individual under the most varied circumstances and conditions, he arrives at a conclusion on this individual's pulse; again, by feeling the pulse of the greatest variety of persons suffering from the same disease, he ascertains the general condition of the pulse under the influence of that disease. It is only then that, feeling a particular patient's pulse, he will be able to judge whether this individual is affected by this peculiar disease, as far as that can be ascertained by its influence on the pulse.

But all these comparisons of the different classes of facts under different local conditions and at different times, of which I have been speaking, depend, not only as to their usefulness and as to the ease with which they can be undertaken, but even as to the possibility of undertaking them at all, on the similarity—nay, congruity—of the method employed, and the expressions, figures, and conditions selected, under which the observations have been taken. Does, then, the world at large not owe the deepest obligations to a Congress such as the one I am addressing, which has made it its special task to produce this assimilation and to place at the command of man the accumulated experience upon his own condition, scientifically elaborated and reduced in a manner to enable the meanest intellect to draw safe conclusions?

Gentlemen, the Congress has at its various meetings succeeded in doing a great deal in this direction: the official statistics of all countries have been improved; and in regard to the Census, the recommendations of the Brussels meeting have been generally carried out in a majority of States. I am sorry to have to admit the existence of some striking exceptions in England in this respect; for instance, the Census of Great Britain and Ireland was not taken on precisely the same plan in essential particulars, thereby diminishing its value for general purposes. The judicial statistics of England and Wales do not show a complete comparative view of the operation of our judicial establishments; nor, while we are in all the departments of the State most actively engaged in the preparation of valuable statistics, can we deny certain defects in our returns, which must be traced to the want of such a central authority or Commission as was recommended by the Congress at Brussels and Paris, to direct, on a general plan, all the great statistical operations to be prepared by the various departments. Such a Commission would be most useful in preparing an annual digest of the Statistics of the United Kingdom, of our widely scattered Colonies, and of our vast Indian empire. From such a digest the most important results could not fail to be elicited.

One of the most useful results of the labours of the Congress has been the common agreement of all States to inquire into the causes of every death, and to return the deaths from the same causes under synonymous names, sanctioned by the Congress. It has in this instance set the example of establishing what is most desirable in all other branches of statistics, namely, the agreement upon well-defined terms. There ought to exist no greater difficulty in arriving at such an agreement in the case of the various crimes than in that of "causes of death;" and it must be remembered that it is one of the first tasks and duties of every science to start with a definition of terms. What is it that is meant by a house, a family, an adult, an educated or an uneducated person; by murder, manslaughter, and so on? It is evident that, as long as a different sense is attached to these terms in different returns, their use for comparison is nil, and for simple study very much deteriorated; and still we have not yet arrived at such a simple and obvious desideratum! The different weights, measures, and currencies in which different statistics are expressed, cause further difficulties and impediments. Suggestions with regard to the removal of these have been made at former meetings, and will no doubt be renewed. We fancy here that our Pound, as the largest available unit, with its Florin, offers great advantages, particularly if further subdivided decimally.

We hope to lay before you, as far as Great Britain is concerned, the Registrar-General's analysis of the causes of death, and the dangers that people encounter at each period of life; complete returns of the produce of our mines;

the agricultural returns of Ireland, in which the Registrar-General of that country has given every year the breadth of land under every kind of crop, with an estimate of its produce as well as its value, and has proved, by his success in obtaining these facts at a comparatively moderate expense, and by the voluntary assistance of the landowners and cultivators, as well as of the clergy of all denominations, that the apprehension was groundless that it could not be done without inordinate cost, or without injuring individual interests. We must hope that, considering its importance with regard to all questions affecting the food of the people, this inquiry will not only be extended to England and Scotland, but also to the Continent generally, wherever it may not already have been instituted. Our trade returns will exhibit the great effects produced on our commerce by the changes in our commercial system; our colonial delegates will exhibit to you proofs of the wonderful progress of their countries, and proofs, at the same time, that elaborate statistics have rendered them conscious of that progress; and I have no doubt that the foreign delegates will more than repay us by the information which they will give us in exchange. These returns will no doubt prove to us afresh, in figures, what we know already from feeling and from experience—how dependent the different nations are upon each other for their progress, for their moral and material prosperity, and that the essential condition of their mutual happiness is the maintenance of peace and good-will amongst each other. Let them still be rivals, but rivals in the noble race of social improvement, in which, although it may be the lot of one to arrive first at the goal, yet all will equally share the prize, all feeling their own powers and strength increase in the healthy competition.

I should detain you longer than I feel justified in doing, and should perhaps trench upon the domain and duties of Presidents of Sections, if I were to allude to the points which will there be specially recommended to your attention and consideration; but I trust that it will not be thought presumptuous in me if I exhort you generally not to lose yourselves in points of minute detail, however tempting and attractive they may be from their intrinsic interest and importance, but to direct your undivided energies to the establishment of those broad principles upon which the common action of different nations can be based, which common action must be effected, if we are to make real progress. I know that this Congress can only suggest and recommend, and that it must ultimately rest with the different Governments to carry out those suggestions. Many previous recommendations, it is true, have been carried out, but many have been left unattended to; and I will not except our own country from blame in this respect. Happy and proud indeed should I feel if this noble gathering should be enabled to lay the solid foundation of an edifice, necessarily slow of construction, and requiring, for generations to come, laborious and persevering exertion, intended as it is for the promotion of human happiness, by leading to the discovery of those eternal laws upon which that universal happiness is dependent!

May He, who has implanted in our hearts a craving after the discovery of truth, and given us our reasoning faculties to the end that we should use them for this discovery, sanctify our efforts and bless them in their results!

LONDON: PRINTED BY W. CLOWES AND SONS, STAMFORD STREET, AND CHARING CROSS.

www.ingramcontent.com/pod-product-compliance
Lightning Source LLC
Chambersburg PA
CBHW032002230426
43672CB00010B/2245